THE YEAR
ZERO

THE YEAR
ZERO

BLAKE

Published by Blake Publishing Ltd,
3 Bramber Court, 2 Bramber Road,
London W14 9PB, England

First published in hardback 2000

ISBN 1 85782 354 0

British Library Cataloguing-in-Publication Data:

A catalogue record for this book is
available from the British Library.

Printed in Great Britain by
Creative Print and Design (Wales),
Ebbw Vale, Gwent.

1 3 5 7 9 10 8 6 4 2

© Text copyright Nicholas Davies
and Dr Matthew Kleinman

Papers used by Blake Publishing Limited are natural, recyclable
products made from wood grown in sustainable forests.
The manufacturing processes conform to the environmental
regulations of the country of origin.

For Antonia and
Cassandra

CONTENTS

ABOUT THE AUTHORS

DR MATTHEW KLEINMAN gained his PhD at
Queen Mary's College, London. He has lectured in
genetics at the University of Hatfield and the Ngee Ann
College, Singapore, and is a mean blues sax player.
He has taken a break from academia to pursue a creative
career in writing, painting and website design.
This is his first book.

Born in England, NICHOLAS DAVIES was educated
privately before being commissioned into the
Royal Warwickshire Regiment after attending Mons
Officer Cadet School. After National Service he served
as a captain in the Sultan of Muscat and Oman's
Private Army.

He is now a highly-respected author and journalist
whose work has been published in countries throughout
the world. Nicholas Davies lives in Surrey with his wife
Andrea and their son, Thomas.

WHAT WAS LIFE LIKE IN BRITAIN TWO THOUSAND YEARS AGO?

AUTHORS' NOTE

This book is an attempt to re-create the lives of the people of Britain in the 80 years between the two Roman invasions, the first by Julius Caesar in the years 55–54BC and the successful invasion of these islands by the Emperor Claudius in AD43.

Much of the evidence of the lives of ancient Britons has been recovered by archaeologists from the remnants of everyday life: broken pottery, fragments of bone, foundations of houses, ditches and banks, pits and holes.

For the most part, we can only guess at the thoughts and feelings of those ancient Britons who then inhabited the island called Albion in those days of pre-history, but it has become possible for historians and archaeologists to decipher the state of the country as it was in that period.

We have endeavoured to reconstruct the lives of its people at that time, seen through the eyes of a young prince, Tasciovanus, who of all the British kings is best known as the father of Cunobelinus whom William Shakespeare made famous as Cymbeline in the play of that name. Cymbeline's grandfather was King Cassivellaunus who ruled over the Catuvellaunian tribe which held sway over much of south-east Britain for generations.

Tasciovanus came to power sometime around 4BC, now generally accepted to have been the year of Christ's birth. Reputedly, Tasciovanus, who was born around 35BC, lived a long and fruitful life and died around AD20.[1]

At first glance, the people who inhabited Albion at that time were living a far more primitive life than the citizens of such sophisticated cities as Alexandria, Athens and Rome. Their art was poor, their architecture undistinguished, their culture fairly basic and their output of anything above the needs of daily life has been mostly lost, if indeed much ever existed.

At that time, the Emperors of Rome and the intelligentsia of Greek and Roman society considered Albion to be a land beyond civilisation, peopled by warring, primitive, illiterate tribes. Greek writers referred to Albion as a mysterious place, a land of spirits, of evil and danger. They wrote stories of strange beasts and

---

[1] There are discrepancies amongst historians as to whether Tasciovanus was the son or grandson of Cassivellaunus. Because of the young age that men fathered children in pre-history Britain, it appears more likely that he was a grandson.

poisonous reptiles roaming the island, of curious religious observances and of savagery and human sacrifices. Albion was considered an unimportant, uninviting island at the outer edge of the world.

We have endeavoured to piece together the everyday lives of the men, women and children of that time, a period of history about which there are no written accounts of the events that shaped Britain or the peoples who lived there. And that is the reason why everything that occurred in England before the Year Zero is described as pre-history.

As a result, it is certain that this book will contain errors, but through careful and diligent research we have endeavoured to reduce these to a minimum.

Nicholas Davies and Matthew Kleinman, April 2000

ACKNOWLEDGEMENTS

A description of life in pre-history Britain and the time of the Roman invasions has to be written with dedicated attention to the meagre literary sources available and all these have been written by those who visited Albion during those years. No written accounts by inhabitants of Britain in the years of pre-history have ever come to light and most historians accept that no such records were ever kept. Julius Caesar was the first person to provide basically accurate descriptions of Albion, its geography, its people and the lives of its inhabitants in his *Gallic War* commentaries.

We have drawn upon the writings of other classical

authors from ancient times, including the Greek traveller Pytheas who visited Britain. We have also sourced other works by such notable writers as Pliny the Elder, Diodorus Siculus, Strabo, Suetonius, Cassius Dio, Ptolemy and the great Roman historian Tacitus. The famous *Letters of Pliny the Younger* have also been extensively used.

We are also indebted to the many modern authors and highly distinguished historians and archaeologists whose work we have diligently read in an effort to re-create the atmosphere of the life and times of pre-history Albion. In particular, we would like to mention the works of such historians as T Rice Holmes, RG Collingwood and J Myers, Gilbert Stone, Peter Salway, Wilfred Bonser, Mommsen, T Hodgkin and HM Scarth. We acknowledge the debt we owe them and others in the extensive bibliography at the end of this book.

We would also particularly like to thank the dedicated staff of the London Library who have kindly helped with stoical research for this project.

1.

THE
ISLAND
RACE

The peasant family living in Britain in Year Zero would have woken in their little round hut, a wigwam-type construction from between 10–20ft in diameter, made from hazel sticks and branches, with the hides of animals attached to the inside to keep out the wind and the rain. Some huts were made of wattle and daub and the entrance was through a low wooden door with a doorstep to keep out water. The whole family, or families, slept on the clay floor on beds of straw covered with animal skins or woollen blankets. To keep warm, the adults and children slept wrapped in the fur of wolves or sheep.

Sleeping in such conditions meant the family stayed warm even in winter, mainly because of the warmth generated by the numbers sleeping there. The floor of the circular hut was usually covered in clay or stone but the poorer families only had straw on the floor. In the centre was a fireplace — a large slab of stone — and there was a hole in the top of the hut for the smoke to escape. Light in the small, overcrowded huts was provided by the flames of the fire and by tallow candles.

In Year Zero, several such huts, sometimes described as beehives, were grouped together to form a settlement or hamlet in which many members of the extended family lived. They shared everything. There may have been simply six or seven such dwellings in one place or, more often than not, 20–30 in which a number of extended families would live together in close proximity.

In some areas of northern Britain, such as Scotland, part of Wales and the Cornish peninsula, families sometimes lived in underground dwellings and caves at this time. These underground habitats generally consisted of a paved trench lined with dry masonry and roofed over with slabs, most ending in a round chamber where the family lived, slept and eat.

There were some families who lived in mound-dwellings, specimens of which were still inhabited in the nineteenth century on the island of Lewis. In some, a central chamber was connected to others and a hole for the smoke was left in the roof which could be opened or closed at will. The chinks between the slabs and stones were stuffed with grass or moss and the roof covered with turf.

The inhabitants of these early dwellings dressed plainly and simply, though the wealthy tribal chiefs who went to war were resplendently kitted out. But for everyday wear, both men and women wore a bright-coloured cloth or linen tunic, a short-sleeved body garment reaching down to the knees. Some tunics were loose-fitting, others more narrow following the contours of the body. And there were rough breeches worn by men, women and children. Some tribes wore the kilt, usually made of multicoloured cloths. No one wore any underwear.

As a protective outer garment for use in the cold, wet weather, both men and women wore a type of cloak fastened on the right shoulder with a brooch. These woollen cloaks, often dyed in bright shades, could be virtually any colour, but following the Roman conquest these cloaks would come to reveal a man's position in life.

The poor peasant, however, usually wore a thin, poor-quality cloak of dull, muddy brown, which would barely keep out a rain shower, let alone a winter deluge. On the other hand, the tribal leader's cloak which he would wear to battle would be a brilliant colour so that he would stand out on the battlefield.

The British men wore their usually fair hair at shoulder length and cultivated long moustaches which drooped down on either side of the mouth. The rest of their faces were closely shaven which was most unusual among tribes throughout Europe. In this respect, the British warrior was a far more striking and unusual figure than his European counterpart who, at that time, nearly all wore beards.

The British men also shaved the rest of their body which in Year Zero was quite profusely hairy. The average height of an ancient Briton at that time was approximately

5ft 6in, while the women were remarkably small, measuring on average two to three inches below 5ft.

The eating habits of the great majority of the serfs, slaves and peasants, who made up 95 per cent of the population, were rudimentary and by the standards of Rome and Athens at that time were indeed barbaric. It was one of the reasons why the then invading Romans dismissed the Britons as 'savage inhabitants'.

There were, of course, no such things as eating utensils in ancient Britain. Nearly everyone — men, women and children — ate their food with their bare hands, ripping meat from the bone and stuffing it into their mouths at great speed as though expecting strangers to arrive at any moment and take it away. Sometimes, the women would chop the meat into smaller pieces for their children using a pocket-knife. The meal would be washed down with large amounts of strong beer drunk from rough earthenware beakers or, in the case of the wealthy, delicately curved silver beakers.

Society was totally male dominated, and life for the great majority of women arduous and tough. Their role included most of the menial tasks which needed to be carried out throughout the year, come rain or shine. Each and every day they had to fetch the water from the nearby stream or pond, collect the firewood, milk the cows, cook the meals, care for the animals — the oxen, horses, cattle, pigs, sheep and deer. They were also required to tend the fields, sowing the wheat and corn and reaping in mid-summer.

The life of a man was equally hard, though not so

tedious. When not at war, defending their villages or attacking their enemies, the men were responsible for constructing defences for the village, ploughing the land, felling the trees and building the huts as well as making swords, spears and shields and the all-important chariots they used when fighting.

Another important role undertaken by the men was as hunter-gatherers, responsible for trapping and killing the wild boars, the deer and wolves and catching fish. The men were also responsible for slaughtering the calves, the sheep and the pigs, the staple diet of all families.

The men also claimed responsibility for rearing the chickens and the cocks, though these were hardly ever eaten. The chickens were customarily used for ritual sacrifices to the myriad of gods the various tribes worshipped, while the cocks were used exclusively for the men's favourite sport, cock-fighting.

Men were also the artisans of the tribe working with wood, metal and stone. They would make the chariots and the harnesses for horses and oxen, the bits and buckles of which were were quite meticulously crafted. Some of the designs they added to the metal parts were delicately and beautifully worked.

And the weapons and shields carried by the wealthier members of society were not mere products churned out by some unskilled ruffian or slave, but were true works of art. It seemed extraordinary to the invading Romans that the British people could live their lives in such primitive dwellings that had originated centuries earlier but, at the same time, could produce the most exquisite art work in every facet of their everyday lives.

Indeed, by the time of Caesar's first invasion of Britain in 55BC, the form of art known as Late Celtic had probably reached its highest point. The artisans who produced these beautifully crafted works of art must have had quite exceptional talent. It seemed that the Britons had concentrated all their artistic skills on working with bronze and other metals. They not only obviously took time and delicate care over making swords and shields with artistic touches but also beautifully worked pots and pans for everyday use. And one way they accentuated the beauty of their work was with the addition of jewels and enamel.

They also produced gilded safety-pins and brooches, bronze and gold rings, bracelets and armlets, necklets and clasps, and bronze and silver mirrors which were often beautifully engraved on the back. Nearly all were well designed and proportioned and were treasured by those who had the good fortune to own them.

When the Romans finally conquered Britain in AD43, they were impressed by the range of art work they found in southern Britain, which they accepted to be as good, if not better, than the art work produced in Rome or Athens at that time. They were also surprised to discover that southern tribes were using inscribed coins to measure value, rather than the weight of metals which the majority of Britons still used in exchange for goods or food.

It revealed to Caesar that at least some of the British — as well as the intellectual Druid priests — could read and write and had even acquired a knowledge of Latin, the mother tongue of the Romans. It suggested to Caesar that

Britain must have had a scholarly culture equal if not superior to what they had discovered during the conquest of Gaul decades earlier.

And yet, if truth be told, the Britain that Caesar twice invaded must have seemed backward indeed compared to the cities of Rome, Athens and Alexandria. He knew all of them well and to the great general it must have seemed like stepping back into a world from one or two centuries earlier. In Year Zero, these great cities were the three major centres of the known world, representing a sophistication unheard of or unseen in ancient Britain.

These cities boasted majestic buildings, paved streets, countless different shops, several markets dealing with all types of food from overseas as well as simply from within Italy. These thriving cities were populated by thousands of people busily going about their daily lives. Every type of trade and skill was practised and the lawyers and architects, doctors and civil servants were well established and in demand. And there was active trade in everything from the four corners of the Roman Empire, including the all-important slave market which drew large crowds most days of the week. There were also thriving industries and artisans working in all known metals, including gold and silver, as well as marble, stone and wood.

The houses of the wealthy were like small palaces with marble floors, tiled walls, bathing pools and, of course, a type of central heating which was remarkably effective. The public buildings included magistrates courts, the senate, debating chambers, and offices for civil servants who ran the Army and the State. And then there was the circus and the truly awesome Roman amphitheatre, where in Year Zero the Roman Empire was indulging its bloodthirsty lust for deadly combat.

The political life of those cities had reached remarkable maturity as well. In Athens, real democracy had been introduced, in which any Athenian could stand for the senate and where every man was entitled to a vote in the city elections. Indeed, the democracy practised in Athens at the time produced a truly representative senate which ignored hereditary class distinctions.

It is also worth considering how far the pure democratic model demonstrated in Athens has come in 2,000 years. Modern Britain claims a 'democratic' form of government, but in reality Britain's alleged democratic process is an oligarchy in which the people are governed by a small group of people of a particular political party. Until recently the two main political parties of Britain did not even choose their leaders democratically. The Conservative Party leader was chosen by a select group reaching an amicable decision over a glass of port, and Labour leader Tony Blair was elected with the help of the union block vote.

In Athens and Rome, there were also public arenas where debates on any subject, including politics, took place, much like Speaker's Corner in Hyde Park today. And there were public areas where slaves, criminals, prisoners of war and even leaders of defeated tribes were brought in chains and either executed or publicly flogged while the crowds looked on, reportedly cheering.

It was at this time that the Roman people enjoyed ever

more visceral pleasures, applauding while Christians were thrown to lions, screaming encouragement as warriors fought each other to the death and cheering on wild animals who were chased into the amphitheatre to tear slaves apart. Indeed, the degradation, humiliation and total disregard shown to slaves in those times reached its height with the public rape of young women slaves at the Roman circus. But little of these gruesome entertainments were known about in ancient Britain.

Just as there was an extraordinary divide between life in 'sophisticated' Rome and that in London in Year Zero, so there was also an enormous disparity in the quality of life between those tribes living in Kent and Essex, which were near the continent of Europe, and those in the northern part of Britain.

Trade had been the great source of education for those living in southern Britain. There were not only trade links across the channel with Gaul, Germany and Scandinavian countries, but also between the south-west of Britain and the western coasts of Gaul and Spain. Trade between Britain and Europe had gone on for centuries but had undoubtedly escalated since Rome had conquered most of western Europe and required a steady supply of the necessities of life, such as an abundance of slaves, wheat, corn and animal hides.

Life was so very different for those tribes living north of a line drawn from the Wash to the Bristol Channel. Even decades into the first century, there were tribes which had not yet learned how to produce bronze or iron or, if they had the knowledge, they had not progressed to making metal implements of any type. Instead, they continued the age-old traditions which had lasted for hundreds of years, working almost exclusively with wood and stone.

Indeed, many tribes, fearful of invaders, had deliberately cut themselves off from any form of social intercourse with outsiders for decades and were still living in the same way as their forefathers had done in the late Bronze Age a thousand years earlier.

People of the interior of Britain, for that is how they are described by some historians, were referred to as 'barbarians' and many referred to them as 'aborigines'. Indeed, to most Britons living in the south, these tribes had never been seen by any living person but knowledge of their existence had been handed down from generation to generation though no one was sure whether the information was factual or the figment of someone's imagination. It transpired 100 years or more after the Roman invasion of Britain in AD43, that there were indeed such tribes and they were found to be very primitive by contemporary standards.

Even by Year Zero, many tribes of the interior did not grow corn, but lived on milk and the flesh of animals and still clothed themselves in animal skins. These small ancient tribes had often settled in the middle of large forests or on the edge of a mountain range and continued their existence with no knowledge of the outside world. And they had usually done so to enable them to live a quiet, peaceful, uninterrupted life, free from attack by marauding warriors or warring tribes.

The chief activity throughout the lives of all ancient

Britons, one which had dominated their every waking moment for centuries, was that of war. And the main fear facing the women of those times was of attack from another tribe or invader.

For centuries before Year Zero, the British Isles had been a natural place in which the tribes and peoples of Europe would settle. Some tribes decided to move to Britain because of the constant state of war many found themselves engaged in on the continent of Europe. They hoped that Britain would offer a more peaceful life for them and their children simply because it was an island, cut off from the mainland.

Despite the fact that Britain was largely a male-dominated culture, the ancient Britons did admit the sovereignty of women. In the middle of the first century, a woman by the name of Cartismandua was queen of the Brigantes and later it was Queen Boudicca, who is better known by her anglicised name of Boadicea, queen of the Iceni tribe, who would lead the courageous rebellion against the Roman conquerors.

Despite this sovereignty, the life of an ordinary peasant woman in the Year Zero was by no means easy. To many, it was horrendous but they knew no better; nor was there any way for them to escape the drudgery, the harsh life, the fact that, to all intents and purposes, they were little more than slaves.

The women, from the moment of puberty until their usually premature death, were the property of the men of the household. Indeed, a hamlet of six or seven huts would, more often than not, consist of all members of an extended family and the girls and the women were the property of the family to be used and abused by every man or boy who lived within the hamlet.[1]

There was no marriage as such among the lower orders who comprised, of course, the vast majority of the population. A young girl would lose her virginity to her own father as a matter of tradition and all her many brothers would then be at liberty to have sex with her. After that initiation to the world of sex, the girl would then be at the beck and call of any man or boy in the hamlet who had the right and the authority to have sex with her at any time they wished.

In fact, all the women of the hamlet would be expected to have sex with whichever man or boy desired them. And there would be no right of denial. From puberty, every woman accepted that any man of the village was entitled to have sex with them whenever they wished, though the head man of the village would always take precedence over the wishes of any other man or boy.

Quite often, a young girl would be offered to a man of another village, but of the same tribe, perhaps in exchange for another girl or one or two animals. Many young girls were bartered for a fast horse which had been trained for use in battle pulling a chariot. On those occasions, all the children that girl produced would automatically be seen as the sons and daughters of the man to whom the girl had been sold and had first been bedded.

The same tradition would apply for girls captured in

[1] It was Julius Caesar who first drew this tradition of wife-sharing to the attention of Rome in his *Commentaries on the Gallic War*, Book V, Chapter XIV.

battle from other tribes. Though the young women may have given birth to one or two children, all her subsequent children would automatically be the children of the man who captured her in battle and who had the right to bed her first. The same rule would also apply to slave girls who had been purchased or bartered. Whichever man first bedded her, all her subsequent children would be the property and responsibility of that man.

In these circumstances, most girls produced their first child by the age of 14 and would then become pregnant usually once a year or so. Of course, miscarriages were prevalent and numerous babies died at birth, or shortly afterwards, but many women would expect to produce ten to fourteen children, many of whom would survive to become adults.

But, the sexual practices of the ancient Britons were even more far-reaching and incestuous. On reaching puberty, every young boy would, by tradition, have his first full sexual experience with his own mother and, only then, would the teenage boy have the right to have sex with his sisters before moving on to other women and their daughters who lived in the village.

As a result, no one ever knew for sure the identity of their fathers though the extended family behaved so much as a single unit that apparently it never seemed to be of any real concern. The women, of course, knew their own children. But all the women acted as mothers to all the children of the village and the men acted as their fathers.

Everyone was called by their given name and the boys

would take the name of their supposed father and would be known as, for example, 'son of John' or whatever the father's name was. There were no surnames. All that mattered was that everyone belonged to the tribal family. No other family unit was necessary.

And there was a very good reason for the extended family to act in unison, caring for each other and each other's children. Life was very, very unpredictable. In the Year Zero, no one knew for sure what would happen from one day to the next. There was no security whatsoever.

If a band of marauding warriors invaded a hamlet, taking the villagers by surprise and putting the men to flight, then the women and children were at their mercy. Usually, the warriors would take away the women they wanted and maybe some of their children, as well as any animals, and then flee as quickly as possible before those defeated villagers could call together other members of the tribe to come to the rescue. As a result, some women changed their habitats, their tribes and their masters perhaps three or four times in a lifetime. It was only when women were old or infirm that marauding warriors left them alone.

Consequently, most villagers would always be on edge, wondering from where to expect the next raid, so shattering their lives, their families, their hamlets and their future. And from a young age, everyone soon accepted that the hamlet's virile young men might die in battle, or be captured and taken away for good and their young, child-bearing women captured and taken off after an inter-tribal raid. It was one of the prime reasons why all the girls and boys, men and women, shared each other sexually to ensure the family continued to produce sufficient babies to keep the tribe going. They knew only too well that without any young, there was no future.

And yet, despite the desperate need to sustain the continuance of the tribe through constant and continuous reproduction, homosexuality was rife among men in ancient Britain but there is no evidence whether women were also involved in such homosexual relationships. Like the basic relationships that existed between the average man and the women in his tribe, which was based almost exclusively on sex, so were the homosexual relationships. But Britain was not alone in this practice for, according to Julius Caesar, the act of homosexuality was common amongst most European countries. Both Strabo and Diodorus wrote of 'unnatural vices' practised by ancient Britons being rife throughout the country. The Greek geographer and philosopher Strabo (60BC–AD20) — whose name means 'squint-eyed' — spent most of his life in travel and study. He explored the Nile and settled in Rome around AD14. His *Geographica* — in seventeen books — is accepted as a bible of facts and observations and was studied by academics for centuries. The Greek Historian Diodorus, who lived in the 1st century BC, travelled throughout Asia and Europe and also settled in Rome. During thirty years of study he collected material for his magnificent *Bibliotheke Historike*, a history of the world in forty books from the Creation to the Gallic wars of Caesar. It was accepted that both Strabo and Diodorus included bestiality in their understanding of the 'unnatural vices' practised by Britons and many other European peoples, but modern historians appear to have fought shy of repeating the suggestion.

Fortunately, for those born around Year Zero the practice of cannibalism was dying out, though it had not altogether disappeared from parts of Cornwall, Wales, Scotland and Ireland.

And life was short and brutal enough for both men and women. Life expectancy for men was around 45 years of age and for women only 35, primarily because of the number of children they bore. Of course, many young women died in childbirth and many young men died in battle. It was a small and vicious circle with little or no release.

Physical conflict — whether it was inter-tribal enmity or resistance against the Romans — brought the most terrible consequences for the vanquished. Some of those men defeated on the field of battle were immediately put to the sword, particularly those who had suffered serious injury. Other men were taken captive, often to be taken to an eastern port and sold to traders as slaves.

The young, well-built, athletic, fair-haired Britons fetched very good money, particularly in Italy where many were shipped in chains. Their destiny would depend on who bought them at market. Some ended their days literally being thrown to the lions in Rome's amphitheatre before a baying crowd of thousands. Others were sold as slaves for a variety of reasons and the more fortunate few ended up as male concubines servicing the wealthy women of Rome.

The slave trade was, without doubt, the main industry,

the principal trade of Europe at this time. There was of course a thriving trade in cattle, sheep, horses and animal furs, and there was an accelerating trade in gold and silver, bronze and iron. In monetary terms, however, the slave trade was the most lucrative. Every country in Europe, north Africa and Mesopotamia was involved in the trade. Tens of thousands of young men captured by the Romans in battle were sent off in chains to various parts of the Roman Empire to be sold into slavery. Some of the strongest men and the best-looking young women were sent to Rome to be sold for the highest prices in the slave markets that were held every week in the city.

And the income from slavery would go to the Emperor's exchequer to help pay for Rome's ambitious overseas invasions. The slave trade would finance the tens of thousands of legionnaires, arm and feed the Roman armies, and cover the astronomical cost of hundreds of ships, thousands of horses and the wagons which the Army used in great numbers.

Income from the slave trade would also help towards the cost of building garrisons overseas, raising regiments of cavalry and paying the thousands of veterans who had retired after decades of fighting for the Empire through many campaigns. In many respects, much of the illustrious Roman Empire was built on slavery and kept going by capturing young men from all corners of the known world.

And, of course, it wasn't only the young men who fetched high prices. Young women, too, were bought and sold and the young British women fetched good prices because their hair was fair and their skin pale, unlike the vast majority of women in the empire who, understandably, were darker skinned with dark hair.

There was, of course, trade in a thousand and one other different items, but the Roman legions were primarily interested in their own needs, which meant they concentrated on trading in wheat and corn, sheep and cattle, hides and furs and, of course, horses.

And in the Year Zero, Britain had all these to offer in abundance.

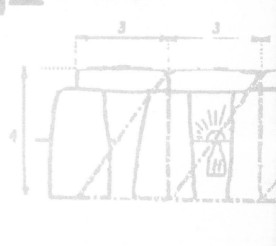

2.

THE PRINCE AND THE PAUPER

Fortunately, there are individuals whose lives have been recorded, real people who lived around the time of Year Zero.

One such man was Tasciovanus, the grandson of Cassivellaunus, leader of the most powerful tribe in Britain who had the rare distinction of being one of the few military leaders to defeat the great general Julius Caesar in at least one memorable battle. Cassivellaunus also claimed that he was responsible for chasing Caesar and his legions out of Britain in both 55BC and 54BC, but that was most certainly an exaggeration, if not a complete fabrication of the events.

Tasciovanus was born some time around 35BC, and

apparently ruled for about fifteen years around the time of Year Zero.

As the grandson of such an illustrious leader, Tasciovanus heard tales of his grandfather's epic victories on the field of battle at first hand for Tasciovanus lived within the extended royal family in the family fortress at Verulam[1] (now St Albans) the capital of the Catuvellauni tribe which held sway throughout the region of modern Hertfordshire and Bedfordshire. It was from this fortified headquarters that Cassivellaunus would lead his formidable forces into the surrounding areas in his determination to capture and hold as much territory as possible. He wanted to be king of the most powerful tribe in Britain.

In some 20 years, Cassivellaunus, undisputed king of the tribe of the Catuvellauni, which had successfully invaded Britain from mainland Europe in around 120BC, achieved remarkable supremacy over many of the primitive tribes which then lived in the regions now known as Hertfordshire, Bedfordshire and Essex.

This rapid success had been achieved mainly through ferocious tactics on the field of battle and enforced subservience to the Catuvellauni tribe of all those other tribes which had been defeated in battle. In particular, the success was attributed to Cassivellaunus, described as a brilliant army commander and dare-devil military tactician,

---

[1] Verulam was renamed by the Romans from the Celtic Verulamium. Similarly, Londinium was renamed London. But after the departure of the Roman forces from British soil around AD446 the British decided the city should keep the short Roman name of London. The earliest mention of London occurs in the *Annals* of the historian Tacitus, describing the events of AD61. He wrote of a busy centre of commerce. London became a wealthy town/city in the last century BC and the first century AD due to a dramatic increase in trade with continental Europe. The conquest of Britain increased that trade still further. London then stood on the hill formed by Tower Hill, Cornhill and Ludgate Hill and with the natural protection of the Fleet, Wallbrook and Thames rivers.

who won the respect of his soldiers by consistently winning battles.

From childhood, Tasciovanus lead a privileged life, growing up in the fortress which his grandfather had built. But this was no great, magnificent, multi-roomed castle but a relatively small, insignificant, single-storey stone building whose primary purpose was to protect the inhabitants from enemies and invaders.

The fortress was protected in the customary manner with a palisade, a barricade of sharpened, up-ended sticks surrounding the whole area, immediately behind which a deep ditch, 12–15ft in depth, had been dug around the entire area which measured some 400m^2. In this area, the peasants and soldiers and their families lived in the same wigwam-type round houses as the vast majority of the population. Such a fortress, though primitive, did provide everyone who lived within its compound some protection from marauding warriors.

The fort itself was constructed of stone and rock and the walls rose to a height of about 12ft above ground level. There were ramparts set on the top of the four walls from where tribesmen could throw their spears and hurl rocks at an enemy that was besieging them. And there were only two entrances to the fort, both of which were guarded by huge, thick wooden doors which could be barred in an emergency. A heavy battering ram would have been necessary for anyone attempting to storm the fort.

Inside the fortress, the rooms led off three sides of the quadrangle and included two main halls used for meetings and for dining. In one corner of each main room was a large hearth with a hole in the ceiling above it for the smoke to disperse. There was also a large kitchen area which boasted hearths below a cooking range, and a large spit capable of roasting a deer above the long hearth. The other 20 or so rooms along the other two walls of the square building were the sleeping quarters for the extended family members, as well as servants' and maids' quarters.

Understandably, wealthy landowners lived in relative comfort and style compared to the average tenant. Most of the tribal land, owned by the nobility and privileged royal retainers, was let out to the rural peasants who lived in a state of semi-serfdom paying their masters in produce and holding back sufficient food for themselves and their family so they would not starve. As ever, it depended on the generosity of the landowner as to how much the serf was permitted to keep back for his family.

During the lifetime of Tasciovanus's grandfather, there was a gradual move towards people congregating into larger villages which, over the next few decades, developed into small towns. The first villages to become quite important centres of life and trade were Verulam (modern St Albans) the capital of the Catuvellaunians; Corinium (Cirencester); Camulodunum (Colchester); and Calleva (Silchester in Hampshire).

Most of these towns were, of course, fortified. London had already become a major centre for trade, but more as a port protected from coastal storms than the important city that it later became under the influence of Rome towards the end of the first century AD. In fact, after the successful invasion of Britain in AD43, the Roman senate wanted

London to be re-named Augusta in honour of the Emperor Augusta who ruled from 27BC to AD14, but the people of Britain had always called the place Londinium and continued to do so until Rome was forced to accept the name.

And the many tribal capitals throughout Britain around the Year Zero were, of course, always fortified but there was a great difference in their size, population and importance. Some were little more than villages surrounded only by a palisade, while more substantial capitals were hill-forts, usually situated in strategic positions on treeless heights commanding a good view of the surrounding countryside. Sometimes these housed just a few people, who were in effect using the fort as a look-out, but some other forts were obviously used by wealthy landowners and chieftains and their extended families who would also have quarters for their slaves, servants and maids.

These wealthy landowners lived in what can only be described as country houses, either the 'corridor' type or the 'courtyard' type. The corridor house consisted of a row of rooms with a passage running between them. They were far from luxurious but most were constructed of rock, stone, daub and wattle, with the floors usually tiled. The courtyard-type consisted of three rows of rooms which formed three sides of a quadrangle.

By the standards of the mass of the population, life in Tasciovanus's fort was pleasant, though certainly not comfortable or luxurious by any stretch of the imagination. Inside the fort, the rooms were sparsely furnished with wooden beds, benches, chairs, stools and tables. There was no water source inside the fort. Like everyone else who lived in their huts surrounding the fort, someone would have to go to the nearby spring, pond or stream to fetch water. And Tasciovanus's diet was virtually no different from that of the peasants — plenty of barely cooked meat with bread, washed down with beer. But during his lifetime, Tasciovanus was fortunate that the amount of trade with Europe increased dramatically and, as a result, his personal diet improved immeasurably as merchants began to import different foods, as well as wine.

For most of his life, Tasciovanus lived the same hard, demanding existence as the great majority of the population who lived within striking distance of the British Channel. For it was in the area of the Home Counties that tribes not only had to withstand the invasion forces from Europe but who were also prone to constant inter-tribal attacks from both old and new enemies. Ambitious tribal leaders, who wanted to lead larger, more powerful armies which were capable of defending themselves from European invaders, believed the way to ensure self-protection was to conquer smaller tribes within their region.

The greater part of Tasciovanus's teenage years was taken up with training to fight with a sword, a staff, a spear and a sling, at the same time as learning defensive techniques with a shield. Each and every day the great majority of the teenage boys of the tribe would gather for instruction from war veterans considered too old to fight. There would be mock battles, wrestling matches, running races and trials of strength and Tasciovanus would be given coaching by a first-class swordsman because he, more than anyone else on the battlefield, would be the enemy's principal target.

Quite often, tribesmen would flee a battlefield *en masse* if their warrior chief was mortally wounded or killed in battle because they believed that was an omen for defeat. And the tribesmen knew what future, if any, awaited them if they were taken prisoner.

His shield, like many others, was more a work of art than a mere protective device. The bronze shield, like those of most other pre-history warriors, was circular in shape and decorated over the whole outer surface with concentric rings, of which some examples boasted up to 30 such rings, separated by circles of small studs. His bronze sword was leaf-shaped, the blade tapering gently inwards from the hilt, then gradually expanding until, at about one-third of the distance from the point, it attained its greatest width. These swords, as well as certain rapier-shaped swords, were intended for stabbing, not striking. They were generally about 60 centimetres long, but others varied between 40 and 75 centimetres in length. The sheaths were made of either leather or wood and tipped with bronze.

The bronze spears used by the British tribes prior to Year Zero were almost identical with neolithic flint weapons. But from Year Zero onwards, the spear-heads were cast in stone or bronze moulds. Some poorer quality spear-heads were cast in clay or compacted sand.

Only when Tasciovanus had mastered the art of swordsmanship and defence was he permitted to face the next important lesson — learning to drive, control and fight from a chariot. The British tribal leaders were almost unique among European tribes in their use of these chariots of war which proved themselves time and again to be the decisive element in many a battlefield victory. Most British commanders led their men from the back of a chariot because they found it easier to direct the troops during a battle if their soldiers could easily see them, instilling confidence.

And Tasciovanus was brought up in the belief that his main duty in life was to be a leader, a gallant, courageous and lucky warrior whom his soldiers and tribesmen would trust to bring battlefield victories and feel so confident in his leadership that they would readily obey.

Tasciovanus was educated and taught to read and write the Celtic language by the Druids whose responsibility it was to educate the nobility, the wealthy landowners and the privileged so they were the better able to handle the affairs of State later in life. His Druid teacher also tutored him in Greek as they themselves had learned to read and write in the ancient classical language. It would be some decades after the conquest of Britain in AD43 that Latin came to supersede Greek as the nation's official second language. Tasciovanus was also taught the history of the tribe which he had to learn by heart and be capable of reciting from memory. The Druids believed that learning by heart was the best way of educating and training the mind to think efficiently.

Unlike the peasants, Tasciovanus was expected to marry, though he would have had little or no choice in the matter. The marriage would probably have taken place when Tasciovanus was 14 years of age. A bride, probably aged 12 or 13, would have been selected for him by his father, a man by the name of Andoco, an abbreviation of his full name which appeared on coins. It is not known what reasons Andoco had for selecting his son's bride, but it was likely to have included a beneficial inter-tribal motive or the offer of a large dowry. Marrying the young Tasciovanus would have been seen as a great privilege and a great honour, much like a girl marrying the Prince of Wales today.

And yet, in pre-history Britain, there was an equality of the sexes but reserved only for those women at the highest level of society, members of the nobility or wealthy landowners. Despite the male domination of family life, female sovereignty was, as we have seen, a fact of tribal life, but instances were few and far between. Cartismandua and Boadicea are the only examples of female leadership. Tasciovanus's bride would also have been permitted to own her property.

Unless the circumstances were exceptional, Tasciovanus would have been expected to add an equivalent amount of property from his own estate and then he would have been responsible for administering the two together as a joint possession. The whole estate and the accumulated increments would then be handed lock, stock and barrel to the survivor of the marriage, and then, of course, to the eldest child of the marriage, either male or female.

But the male of the species had the whip hand. Tasciovanus, as any other husband in those days of pre-history, had the power of life and death over his wife as well as over his children. But he could not summarily announce that he had decided to execute his wife. He would have had to argue his decision and debate the matter with his advisers, the Druids, who, though they had no absolute power, held the greatest influence over the kings, princes, war lords and tribal chiefs. If they came to the conclusion that his wife was not blameworthy or culpable of any serious misdemeanour, then it would be most unlikely that the king would be permitted to go through with his decision.

But there was danger in death for a king's widow. If there were any suspicious circumstances surrounding Tasciovanus's death, members of his immediate family had the right to question and cross-examine his widow, flog her and torture her if necessary, in an effort to discover the truth. This rough justice took place within 24 hours of the king's death, so that if the wife was found guilty of contributing in any way to her husband's death, she would be condemned to perish in the flames of her husband's funeral pyre.

Throughout his marriage Tasciovanus was permitted to keep as many concubines as he wished, and any children of such unions were accepted as his children but only those sons and daughters by his wife were entitled to succeed him as king of the tribe. Nonetheless, the fortunate bastard children enjoyed the privileges of life which they shared with the king's legitimate children.

It is believed that Tasciovanus succeeded his father as king in around 4BC, the same year as it has become accepted that Jesus Christ was born, and died around the year AD20, some 23 years before the successful Roman conquest of Britain. In those days, a 25-year reign was seen as a remarkable achievement, primarily because of the king's role as the tribe's commander and war lord and the many battles he would have had to have survived throughout his reign.

In fact, Tasciovanus and other kings of that period were really commanders-in-chief of their Armies, war lords responsible for protecting the kingdom and enhancing the reputation and territory of the tribe. Tasciovanus had very little to do with actually organising the affairs of the tribe. The people responsible for advising Tasciovanus and making tribal policy were mainly the Druids, the wise men, who sat as a sort of cabinet. They would take it upon themselves to plan policy, adjudicate in tribal arguments, and advise on the necessary defences for the tribe. They would then appraise the king of their ideas and their considered advice and he would make the final decision. But, of course, under such circumstances, Tasciovanus came to rely on his faithful Druids to a great degree, though they never forgot that he was the king, the ruler.

The majority of Tasciovanus's life was spent hunting for pleasure, training for war or leading his warriors in battle. It was surprising that he lived such a long life.

Tasciovanus cut a dashing figure when he rode out in his two-horse chariot at the head of his Army, his shoulder-length fair hair blowing in the wind, his long crimson cloak clasped by a coral-studded brooch, his sword clanking in its decorated scabbard, his bronze shield gleaming like gold and adorned with enamel, his horse's bridle shimmering with enamelled cheek-pieces and the harness jangling with open-work bronze ornaments.

Like any king, Tasciovanus employed trusted retainers, usually other military commanders and nobles within the Catuvellauni tribe who owed their allegiance and their position to him. Tasciovanus enjoyed a long and prosperous reign and was responsible for forging many smaller tribes under his leadership. Throughout the 50 years on either side of the Year Zero, dramatic changes took place in southern and eastern Britain with tribes being brought together in bigger and bigger communities.

But it is likely that Tasciovanus knew very little of the ethnic background of his tribe nor the relationship of his tribe to other tribes within Britain. The island's first inhabitants were believed to have belonged to the Neanderthal stock, recognisable by their retiring foreheads and large brow-ridges. The neolithic invaders of the later Stone Age — when man first used polished stone implements and weapons — arrived from Gaul and spread throughout the British Isles. Over the next 1,000 years, various peoples from Germany, Spain and the Low Countries filtered into Britain and mixed with the peoples they found already living there. The first Celtic invaders were called Goidels — originally from Scotland and Ireland — who had reached Ireland centuries before.

The first Gaulish immigrants from Brython — the Celtic name from which the word Britain was taken — inaugurated the Iron Age in Britain. They were succeeded by the Belgae who came mainly from the Low Countries.

The Picts were a medley of different tribes from the continent, including Celts, with whom they had inter-married long before moving to Britain. And the north of England, except Humberside, became occupied by a people known as the Brigantes who had emigrated from Europe. Their lives were comparatively peaceful until the Romans decided to conquer the north of the country.

Everywhere in Britain, the pre-Roman stocks have, in greater or lesser proportions, survived to this very day. The vast majority of today's Englishmen, Welshmen or Scotsmen, if their pedigrees could be traced back far enough, could be found to count among their ancestors men of the type who were buried in pre-history barrows (mounds), sturdy warriors of the Bronze Age, and Celts who fought against Caesar or were subdued by Agricola.

Tasciovanus must have followed in his grandfather's footsteps, gaining a great reputation for himself within the Catuvellaunian tribe because during his reign he succeeded in establishing the tribe far beyond the area carved out by his grandfather. By the end of his reign, Tasciovanus ruled over a region which included modern Essex and Northamptonshire, as well as the whole of the country north of the Thames, as far west as Gloucestershire and Oxfordshire in the north. There had never been another tribe which held dominion over such a vast area at any time in pre-history Britain.

And the only way in which Tasciovanus could have established control over such a vast area would have been by winning great victories on the battlefield.

Apparently, Tasciovanus produced many children, but

one in particular — a boy by the name of Cunobelinus — would attain lasting fame and immortality under the name Cymbeline, given him by William Shakespeare. It appears that much of Shakespeare's play was based on fact.

Cymbeline was King of the Catuvellauni and he did marry a widow who had a son by her former husband, whom Shakespeare named Cloten. King Cymbeline wanted his daughter Imogen to marry Cloten, but she was already married. So, Cymbeline banishes the husband to Rome. The tortuous love story, woven so brilliantly by Shakespeare, ends with Imogen reunited with her beloved husband but only after alleged adulteries, poisoned potions and timely deaths. Interestingly, Cymbeline not only gives his blessing to the two lovers but also restores peace between the British and the Romans.

There was also an important historical point in Shakespeare's play made in a statement by Geoffrey Monmouth that Cunobelinus (Cymbeline) was educated by the Emperor Augustus. The silver and copper coins struck in the King's name revealed the growing influence of Roman culture, and many were undoubtedly designed by Romans or artists who had received Roman training. It had been suggested that Cunobelinus was sent to Rome by his father where he adopted many Roman ways, including the exquisite workmanship of coins.

Tasciovanus must have died a contented man having achieved every goal his father had set him. Aided by his many sons, including Cunobelinus, the Catuvellaunian Army had conquered the Trinovantes, their great rivals and arch enemies of nearly 100 years, annexing their territory.

This conquest made the Catuvellaunians the greatest and most powerful tribe in Britain and earned Cunobelinus the unofficial title given him by the Romans of the first 'King of Britain'.

But there were also paupers.

Indeed, the vast majority of the 500,000 or so inhabitants of southern Britain — the most populated part of the country around the Year Zero — lived a harsh, miserable existence.

There was a slave who lived around the Year Zero, a man of the same tribe as Tasciovanus, whose name appears to have been Severus. His life changed dramatically at a young age when his father had been killed and his young mother had been taken by a rival tribe, the Dobini, whose territorial dominions covered today's Somerset and Gloucestershire. His mother was taken as a concubine by one of the warriors and would never again return to her own tribe.

Severus was brought up as a young slave with no privileges and little hope of any future. He worked on the farms, carrying out all the menial tasks that were assigned to young lads. In return, he would be given a meal a day, usually meat and bread and somewhere to lay his head. But the round-houses the slaves lived in were squalid, over-crowded shacks, unfit for human occupation. His clothing would have been the barest minimum, probably old rags thrown out by the poor labourers themselves. As in Rome at this time, slaves were not individuals with any rights but objects to be bought and sold whose owners had absolute authority over their destiny.

He may have thought a better life lay ahead when he heard he was to be sold. He hoped his new life would be a change for the better from the drudgery and mindless violence he had to endure working as a farm labourer where beatings were dealt out for little or no reason. But they occurred very frequently.

Indeed, most slaves were treated as little more than dogs, regularly beaten with sticks or whips for the least transgression.

Young Severus was sold on from the Dobini tribe following his mother's death. He was taken to work in the lead mines in the Mendips, a brutal existence where every man in the mine was a slave, compelled to work long hours in the most appalling and dangerous conditions from which there was no hope of escape.

There is no knowledge of what happened to poor Severus but his life was probably short, and brutal.

The conditions in which he was forced to live were undeniably appalling, made worse by the discipline imposed by those who owned the mines, where slaves were treated more like beasts of burden than human beings. The received wisdom among such mine owners at that time was that the slaves who worked in the mines would work harder and faster the more they were beaten. Those slaves who decided to try to escape were, more often than not, quickly found and brought back to face a public flogging in front of all the other slaves as a warning to them not to attempt similar bids for freedom.

Each day, the slaves would work from dawn until dusk and there was no respite at weekends. Their living accommodation was often in the mines which were at least warm in winter, but the sleeping conditions were intolerable with only straw for bedding and no covering save for the filthy clothes they worked in. Food was minimal — meat, bread and water — and no beer was permitted.

It was no life, only a matter of survival, with the hope that one day they would be granted their freedom. But in ancient Britain this was a rare event, especially if the men were working in mines or on the land. Many workers died in their early thirties, worn down and worn out by the heavy workload they were forced to undertake each and every day of their lives.

The more fortunate slaves were those employed in the homes of the wealthy and the nobility, but even then slaves were regularly beaten or whipped for the most trifling of misdemeanours, such as overcooking the food or dropping something on the floor.

Generally speaking, slave girls were treated somewhat better than their male counterparts. Most worked hard on the land where the conditions were oppressive and pitiless. Many women were bought by their wealthy owners to work in the kitchens. And young women from the age of 12 were frequently purchased as concubines but, when they were no longer wanted, they were usually sent off to work in the fields. But they, too, did not escape the tyranny of slavery nor the heavy-handed punishment meted out through regular beatings.

The children of slaves faced an uncertain future, depending on the status of the mother within the owner's household. So far as is known, however, no children of such relationships were ever accepted by the father as his legal descendants. Their future would depend on the generosity, or otherwise, of the woman's owner. Many such children were also brought up as slaves and would never know a life outside the bonds of slavery.

Some slaves managed to persuade their owners to permit them to serve in the tribe's Army, particularly if they showed skill as archers, slingers or swordsmen. There were also some fortunate slaves, but they were very few and far between. These were the most intelligent slaves whom their owners realised could be put to better use than working in the fields or the kitchens. These slaves were usually artisans, youngsters who had shown a talent as leather workers, engravers, metal workers or masons.

The life of a slave in ancient Britain was no worse and no better than that of a slave anywhere else in the known world, but the lives and conditions of most slaves did improve after Roman legions had conquered their area or their country. This was because, to a certain degree, the Roman Empire was built and maintained on the foundations of a highly organised slave trade, in which slaves were granted a legal status.

The main drawback, however, was the fact that the Roman legions were obliged to capture and send back to Rome hundreds and, on occasions, thousands of slaves who would then be sold at market. These men and women would never again set foot in Britain or see their families. Despite the dreadful and harsh conditions which many slaves endured in Britain, there was, quite naturally, the fear of the unknown. Terrifying tales had filtered back to Britain through traders, telling of slaves being fed to wild animals such as lions — an animal which, of course, no one in Britain had ever seen.

But such a fate would, more than likely, have struck fear in those wretched slaves who were taken away from Britain to an unknown future. The men were usually soldiers who had been defeated in battle, but some slaves were usually offered by defeated commanders as substitutes. Understandably, the commanders wanted to keep their warriors. Sometimes, Roman generals would take any hostages offered, whether soldiers or former slaves. But their future would be bleak indeed.

They would usually be marched to a British port on the south-east coast from where they would be handed over. They would then be packed into the holds of ships, rather like sheep and cattle are transported in ships today. On arrival in Gaul, they would then have to walk to the nearest slave market or, for the majority, they would have to walk to Rome, a distance of some 700 miles!

Despite such a fate, the Roman conquest of Britain came as something of a relief to many slaves because, under Roman law, it was accepted that a slave could one day earn his or her freedom and become a 'freedman' or 'freedwoman'.

Such freedom was usually offered to a slave by their master on reaching the age of 30, but not always. There was no automatic right of freedom. Once again, such a privilege was only in the gift of the owner. That right could not necessarily be earned either, though many slaves believed that good, dutiful behaviour to their owner would help win their freedom.

However, even after being granted their freedom, slaves continued to have a legal relationship with their former owners. After obtaining their freedom, the relationship between slave and master would, usually, change dramatically. Slaves often felt bound to their masters in the same way as a monk may feel bound to his abbot or a junior to his barrister. Most Roman slaves came to accept that slavery was simply an institution to which they belonged. It was their station in life, not necessarily that he, or she, was the helpless victim of a more powerful force.

In Rome, highly intelligent slaves who had proved their worth could become civil servants working for the State. The most powerful former slaves became 'imperial freedmen' in the Roman Empire, in effect, senior civil servants with highly responsible positions. Indeed, one such former slave, a man by the name of Polyclitus, was sent by Rome during the first century to investigate a dispute at the top level of the Roman administration in Britain. As he was ordered to do so by the Emperor, Polyclitus was permitted to take an enormous entourage to Britain, travelling in great style. Once in Britain, he was treated with the greatest respect.

3.

FARMING

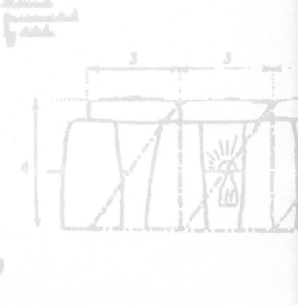

It was mainly the women of the hamlets who were responsible for carrying out most of the farm work, as they had done for the previous 500 years throughout the Iron Age. Throughout those centuries, very little had changed to alter the hard grind of their daily lives which, of course, never ended. There were no such events as weekends or holidays, and no days off unless they were struck down with some debilitating illness.

Shortly after dawn, they would awake in their bare, draughty, little round-houses, and know for certain what lay ahead that day. In an effort to keep out the cold and the wind, they had attached leather hides with hemp to the inside of the wooden-framed houses, but that would probably have made little difference.

Their night's rest would not exactly have been comfortable, lying on straw bedding on the clay floor. In the summer, their huts and the straw and animal furs on which they lay would have been infested with flies, bedbugs, lice, fleas and probably many other species of insect. Only in the summer would they take out the straw and burn it, replacing it with fresh straw which would last another 12 months.

Nobody bothered to wash except during the summer when the villagers would splash around in a nearby pond or stream to keep cool in the heat. As a result, there was a constant fetid stench in the huts which those that inhabited them would hardly have noticed because they were so used to the smell, though outside the air would have been always fresh and clean.

The women would throw off their coverlets, usually made from wolfskin or sheepskin and, dressed in nothing but a ragged, colourless, one-piece woollen garment, the shape of a full-length tunic, they would take care of their babies and children, feeding them milk and readying them for the day. Indeed, feeding the young children would have been a job-and-a-half because most of the women produced babies at the rate of one a year after puberty.

Only then would they make their way out to check to see if the livestock were in good shape. If there was heavy rain the women would throw a hide over their shoulders and tie it with leather strips around their necks. Most of the women wore nothing on their feet, others would simply wrap their feet in cloth in an attempt to keep out the dew, the wet or the cold, while the less impoverished women would wear coarse, open leather sandals.

There would be little variation in their routine daily chores come rain or shine. The women would milk the cows and the goats and return to the round-house where a number of men, women and older children, who all lived together under one roof, would break their nightly fast eating bread and drinking beer, milk or water.

The same early morning ritual would take place in all the other homes of the hamlet that were usually built within a few yards of each other forming the nucleus of a small, intimate community, as well as helping each other in defending the hamlet against the all-too frequent raiders.

Indeed, the women bore the brunt of the great majority of the daily work routine. They would not only be responsible for taking care of the farm animals but would also tend the fields, sow and reap the harvest, collect firewood, make and stoke the fires, cook all the meals and, of course, take care of the babies and the children. The women who lived together under one roof would work as a team with the younger women having the various responsibilities allotted to them by the senior matriarch of the extended family who wielded considerable authority.

For many decades, if not centuries, before Tasciovanus was born, farm livestock consisted principally of pigs, goats, sheep and cattle and, in some circumstances, deer. Some villages kept both red and roe deer in small herds in areas not far from the hamlet for they were useful principally both for their meat and their hides, which were put to all manner of uses.

Cattle and oxen were kept to pull carts and the rudimentary form of ploughs used to till the land. Horses were considered too much of a luxury to be used for ploughing. Most serfs never owned any horses for that reason. But the more well-to-do villages had begun to keep horses, though these were mainly used for hunting.

As a result, more often than not, small-boned bullocks were used on the land because they proved easy to handle and control. In tiny hamlets, however, where perhaps only two or three extended families lived together, cows were generally preferred because they could not only pull carts and other farm implements but would, at the same time, provide the necessary supply of milk.

From Iron Age times, both bullocks and cows had been used in pairs and were yoked in one of two ways, either neck-yoked or horn-yoked. Arguments over the two methods of yoking, as a means of controlling the cattle, were hotly disputed by generations of farmers and it was an issue which was not resolved for centuries, although neck-yoking would eventually become the norm.

The principal cattle were shorthorns, small rangy animals which were able to survive on mean pasture and capable of withstanding harsh winters on meagre food supplies. They were also capable of providing an adequate milk supply for two or three families. Most importantly, these hardened cattle were amenable to the yoke and would sometimes become more of a household pet than a farm animal.

In some of the smaller hamlets, with perhaps just two or three round-houses clustered together, the one or two cattle would often be housed at night with the extended family in the main dwelling, sharing the large single room. But in the larger hamlets, with numbers of families living nearby, they would usually be housed in makeshift byres adjacent to the houses. In this way, the precious cows could be more easily guarded from rustlers.

During the day, the cattle were taken from their shelter and tethered in a suitable grazing area nearby where they would be moved throughout the day so there would always be a plentiful supply of grazing. Other families would tether their cattle and bring hay to them every few hours, a more laborious method but it did ensure that families could keep a protective eye on their precious livestock.

Principally, the decision to establish hamlets was dictated by the quality of the land immediately surrounding the proposed site. To be near good arable land was essential, but there also had to be areas within close walking distance where animals could safely graze. The hamlets also needed to be settled near running water. In the Year Zero, agriculture was still the only means of survival for the vast majority of the tiny population of Britain which then probably numbered little more than half a million men, women and children.

Many peasants at that time, as well as their fathers and forefathers before them, had spent back-breaking years clearing the farms of trees and woodland on which the hamlets and villages now settled. Most of Britain, like the rest of northern Europe, had been covered by forests of various trees which was the principal reason why those who lived in the centuries before were principally hunter-gatherers.

The farming of crops from seed was a dramatic innovation and brought a sea-change to the lives of peasants and reinforced the need for families and extended families to live together in one place so they could farm the land effectively. The need for families and communities to work together brought about the small settlements that eventually became hamlets and villages.

In the past, families would move from place to place, searching for new areas where they could hunt animals in their search for food. But settling down in one place, although it made for a more settled life, particularly for the womenfolk, also brought unforeseen problems.

Some marauders preferred the nomadic life and found in the settlements a ready supply of animals which they could steal and take back to their families. As a result, peasants came to realise that settling close to a number of other families brought protection. Raiders became an ever-present menace, descending out of nowhere to plunder cattle and other livestock, leaving the poor hamlets in a desperate plight.

Raiders, even from hamlets only a few miles away, would sometimes try to steal the livestock even if the best bulls and rams were branded. Those men who were in command of the smaller hamlets would think twice before attempting to recover their livestock from more powerful neighbours for fear of retaliation which could sometimes be swift, ruthless and frequently fatal.

Though life for the peasants and serfs in Year Zero had changed, it was the women who bore the brunt of the daily drudgery of their new life. They were made responsible for working the farms, feeding the livestock, tending the crops and providing food for the animals throughout the year. The men would help in the hay-making, would chop down the trees, construct the round-houses and work at the leather and metal harnesses for the horses and oxen. But the women were responsible for most of the other farming activities.

The farm animals were the very lifeblood of the families and, as a consequence, making and storing sufficient hay to provide food during the long, hard winter months, which were still arduous even in the south of the country in Year Zero, was a most necessary aspect of their work. That meant, of course, that in order to prosper, the hamlets needed good quality land to produce the hay year in, year out.

The women's labour, tilling and ploughing the land was hard and back-breaking work, mainly because of the poor-quality tools available. Tasciovanus would see the women bent almost double over their ancient wooden ploughs, called ards[1]. These ploughs were spiked implements which scored a furrow in the ground, breaking up the soil. These were an efficient tool, the direct modern parallel being the well-known chisel plough, but the women needed strong arms and backs to operate them effectively.

For centuries, these ploughs would be used throughout Britain because they were capable of dealing with not only the light soils of the chalk and limestone uplands but also the heavy clays and loams of the valleys. There was only one major problem — the solid, seasoned oak spikes were worn away by as much as 2.5cm after just half a hectare of ploughing. The arrival of shaped iron spikes to fit over the wooden end of the chisel plough ensured centuries of efficient ploughing.

Pigs were kept domestically by the women and wild pigs and boars were hunted by the men. Both these domesticated pigs and the wild ones were extremely fast and could easily

---

[1] Ards — Ploughs that are not fitted with a mould board, which inverts the soil.

outrun the dogs which hunted them. Some hamlet women also used pigs as an alternative to the plough, which made their work far less arduous. The pigs would be put into a field to prepare and manure a seed bed and, later, to clean up after a harvest. The only human work would entail planting and reaping, which were much less back-breaking tasks.

Sheep were, of course, a vital necessity to all the ancient tribes of Britain, so cold were the winters, particularly north of the Thames and up towards the Pennine mountain range. These sheep were very different from today's docile, slow-moving flocks.

The sheep Tasciovanus saw every day of his life looked more like goats, running with the speed of deer and capable of jumping 1.8m obstacles. These sheep also proved resistant to any control by dogs, and would roam where they wished, though they would always stay around good pastures. In winter, they would usually return to the hamlet in the knowledge that hay would be provided. Their wool was plucked, again by the women, once a year, for the art of shearing had not then been developed. On average, the sheep yielded approximately 1kg of wool per animal per year, meaning that 20 sheep would yield enough to clothe a family of five.

Indeed, so intractable were the ancient sheep that goats were sometimes preferred. Though their coats were of little use for clothing, the goats did yield a good supply of milk, which was never possible from the sheep. The goats were also far easier to domesticate and feed. And they proved useful in clearing ground destined for a hay crop, for they could clear out all the thistles and weeds and yet do little or no damage to the crop itself.

The fact that the goats and the sheep looked so similar was thought to be the original reason for the phrase 'separating the sheep from the goats'!

To Tasciovanus and those young men whose lives were spent hunting and fighting, the horse was by far and away the most important animal on the farm. But the horse of the Year Zero was more like a small Exmoor or Dartmoor pony, some 14 hands high at best, rugged, tough and quite stockily built but, compared to today's horses, not at all fast. They were, however, remarkably nimble.

It is not known for certain whether any fowl were kept on farms in pre-Roman Britain but, if there were indeed some, it is likely the birds were the Indian Red Jungle variety or, alternatively the Old English Game Fowl. There may also have been both geese and ducks, but these also cannot be definitely specified, one reason being that the bones of such birds are so delicate and small that hardly any could have survived from those times.

Farming was, in reality, the only means of survival for the great majority of ancient Britons in Year Zero and, as a consequence, crops were vitally important. If the crops failed, for whatever reason, near disaster would face those families of the hamlet that farmed them.

Of course, they could survive on eating meat or catching fish in the rivers and lakes, but the fact that the crops had failed would mean there was no winter feed for the animals which would, more likely than not, starve to death during the freezing months. Such a calamity would mean that the entire hamlet would find life extremely difficult for at least the following year, when the families would hope that the subsequent crop would produce good yields and save them.

A number of different cereals were grown by the more adventurous hamlets even before the arrival of the Roman conquerors. Certainly two different strains of wheat were grown and, of course, a stylised ear of Emmer wheat — the emblem of the farm — was to be found on the earliest Iron Age coins ever minted in Britain.

Emmer wheat seemed to have found its way to Iron Age Britain from Egypt or some other Middle-Eastern land where it had been successfully grown for many centuries, if not thousands of years. The Roman Army lived and marched on bread made from Emmer wheat because of its high protein value.

And, certainly a century or so before Year Zero, farmers had learned how to sow and farm barley, from which their alcohol — strong, dark beer — was produced. Where the barley was originally imported from is not known but, more than likely, that also came from the Middle East.

Among the men — and some of the women — beer was very popular and drunk in large quantities on a daily basis. It would have helped to relieve the strains, muscle aches and tensions of the hard-worked men and women and facilitate a deep sleep. But the morning would probably have brought major hangovers.

However, it was the successful planting of wheat seed which was responsible, more than any other factor, for bringing about the dramatic change in the lifestyle of Iron Age Britons, changing society from nomadic hunter-gatherers to a nation of settled farmers. Within the space of a hundred years, the landscape had changed dramatically, particularly in southern and eastern Britain, as the forests and woods were decimated, making way for fields in which wheat was sown, harvested and turned into bread or bartered for animals.

The wheat, barley and corn were also bartered for bronze and iron implements which were then being manufactured and, of course, the new iron farm tools were a major step forward in productive farming.

The problems of all hunter-gatherer societies, especially in cold weather climates, had been to secure the satisfactory and sufficient supply of winter food for both humans and the animals the society depended on. The introduction of wheat production meant the farmer and his family had to remain in one locality, hunting game and gathering wild fruits in the spring and summer with the knowledge, and the confidence that instilled, that winter feed for the animals would be secure.

One major problem facing Iron Age farmers was successful seed sowing. The Roman method of distributing seed merely by throwing it on the surface of the soil and then turning the earth would have not been very efficient in a country like Albion where birds were ever-present. As a result, ancient Britons adopted another idea from the Middle East, the sowing-stick, a hockey stick–type piece of carved wood which could easily be pulled along the ground making a shallow seed furrow. It saved precious seed and made for easier and more reliable wheat distribution.

It seemed that another arduous, back-breaking task undertaken exclusively by the women of the hamlets was reaping the ear of the cereals at harvest time, for the cereals grew like plants, all at varying heights making reaping a very

[1] Spar-hooks — Small crescent-shaped blades with a wooden handle used for cutting brambles and splitting wooden rods.

difficult and time-consuming task. In Year Zero, sickles and spar-hooks[1] were used by some farmers but not the majority because picking the ears by hand resulted in a bigger harvest.

The planting of wheat and any other crops also necessitated the building of brushwood fences to surround the crops and keep out predators, whether they were roaming deer, pigs, goats or sheep, which could decimate the crops within a short time. Fence building was a job undertaken by the men of the hamlet. It seemed that though the deer and the goats could easily jump the low fences surrounding the small fields of crops, they did not attempt to for there was food to be found as they roamed the surrounding countryside.

The Celtic bean, a nutritious food with a nutty taste, also became part of the staple diet. The common vetch, a plant of the pea family, which bears a blue flower, provided edible fruit for man and a late herbage crop for animals. Flax, which also produces a blue-coloured flower, was also available to late Iron Age farmers. The stalk of this plant provided linen for clothes by retting, the leaves provided fodder for the farm animals and oil was produced by crushing the seeds — altogether a most productive and efficient plant.

To produce the linen, however, required the digging of huge pits in which the flax could be soaked. These bath-shaped pits, usually lined with clay, required two weeks or more of hard work for five or six men. The heavy, cumbersome shovels of that time were inefficient compared to the spades and shovels of today, especially those that were for the most part still made entirely of wood. During retting[1], the

[1] Flax-retting — The process of preparing flax for making linen by soaking or watering.
[2] Neither spinach nor cabbage was introduced into until Britain some centuries later. Fat Hen was the principal main green vegetable.

stalks of the flax plant were soaked in water for ten days or so before being crushed, soaked for a further period and then combed out over spikes to extract the linen thread. The flax seeds were crushed and put to a large number of uses including, of course, cooking and lighting.

Fat Hen[2] was another plant grown in pre-history Britain which provided a valuable source of nutrients to the villagers. Cattle, sheep and goats found the leaves most palatable and the pigs consumed it greedily. In some places, Fat Hen would be called 'pig weed' or 'hog weed'.

One of the great advantages of Fat Hen was the short time it took from sowing to reaping the crop. If a cereal crop failed, because of unduly dry, hot or wet weather, Fat Hen could be sown and a valuable crop obtained within four months providing vital late fodder for the farm animals and seed for the women to grind into flour. The flour would be used during the winter months to make bread.

One of the tasks reserved for men was the construction of storage pits. These pits, of varying shapes and sizes, were used for a variety of purposes. Some were 3m deep and 1m wide but others were far smaller. Some would be lined with clay, others lined with basketwork, while the great majority would be left hewn out of the chalk, sand or the limestone of the area.

These pits were used for storing many products, such as water and hides, but were principally reserved for the storage of foodstuffs, mainly grain. Once again, it seems the idea of using underground storage pits came from the Middle East where wheat had been stored in similar pits in the dry heat of the area for generations. In Britain, problems sometimes arose in grain storage pits because the damp and moisture would sometimes have a damaging effect on the grain. Despite this, storage pits became the accepted way of storing grain and other crops.

Leather tanners and potters, too, would use the pits. The potters needed pits in which to wash the clay and to mature it prior to forming it into pots, plates and bowls.

As a result, the greater the number of people who came to live in a hamlet or village and who took part in working the farms and producing and caring for the livestock and the crops, the greater the number of pits required. In some areas of southern Britain, sometimes as many as 100 pits would be sunk within a few square kilometres. And that was simply because, by the Year Zero, the production of wheat and other crops was developing rapidly and huge areas of land were being cleared and sown.

Within a matter of a few decades, before Julius Caesar's first invasion of Britain in 55BC, Tasciovanus's tribe, the Catuvellauni, were bartering and selling wheat by the shipload to the Roman Armies then living across the channel, mainly in southern Gaul. The Roman generals needed good quality wheat for their tens of thousands of soldiers who were stationed in both Gaul and the lands east of the River Rhine. When good quality wheat began to arrive from Britain during the early part of that century, more was requested, ordered and delivered.

The powerful Roman generals, operating at the behest of the Roman Emperor, were provided with generous funds enabling them to pay handsomely for plentiful supplies of good quality wheat. Many of the innovations introduced into

Britain during that century arrived as a direct result of the exchange of knowledge, ideas and farming practice between the traders of Gaul and Britain.

The wealth generated by the increase in trade encouraged such men as Tasciovanus's grandfather, Cassivellaunus, to import numerous other ideas and objects — from body armour to more deadly weapons — which had never before been seen in Britain.

As a result, throughout the century before the successful invasion of AD43, there was a rapid development and sophistication among the upper echelons of the various tribes in the southern and eastern areas of Britain, the ones closest to Gaul. In the areas north of Verulam (St Albans) and west of the River Severn, life continued as it had done for centuries, touched by only very few of the advances which were being rapidly introduced to the southern and eastern areas of the country.

And most of these advances had been brought about by the hunter-gatherers of southern Britain who keenly grasped the new technology of farming the land and, as a result, forging a new life in which they came together to live in settlements, hamlets and villages. In time, towns and cities would follow, as they had done in the Greek and Roman empires.

4.

RELIGION–
THE POWER
OF THE
DRUIDS

Throughout the life of Tasciovanus, the Druids played an important role, having done so for many centuries in pagan Britain. The young prince was educated and tutored by a Druid as his father and grandfather before him. Druid priests would become Tasciovanus's trusted advisers who held great sway with him as they had done with most monarchs and tribal chiefs who then ruled the various parts of ancient Britain.

In many respects, Tasciovanus, and all other tribal chiefs, were principally war lords, the commanders-in-chief of their armies, while the Druids took care of all the other concerns of the tribe, acting as advisers, judges, legal experts and undertaking many other tasks.

In effect, the Druids were the men and, to a lesser extent, the women, who ran Britain's hundreds of ancient tribes and had done so for centuries. They were wise men who placed great faith and many years of study in educating the next generation of Druids, and the nobility, continuing the traditions that had been responsible for civilising ancient Britain.

In effect, they were the intelligentsia, respected for their wisdom not only in Britain but in the far more developed centres of education and learning such as Rome, Athens, Alexandria and parts of Mesopotamia.

The Druids were also respected as prophets and philosophers, poets and seers, lawyers and doctors. Tasciovanus would see Druid priests and priestesses going about their tasks every day of his life. The Druids would also conduct tribal rituals such as baptism and funerals and invigilate at pagan ceremonies including animal sacrifices.

More importantly, the Druids would spend their days teaching the few privileged children of the tribe to learn the facts of Druid history and traditions, insisting that the children learn everything by heart for nothing was ever written down.

Animal sacrifices had been a routine ritual in tribal life for centuries and, on special occasions, human sacrifices were offered to the gods. On such occasions, Druid priests would watch over the events but hardly ever took an active part. It was as if the Druids were attending as official witnesses while others actually conducted the gruesome affairs.

Tasciovanus would have witnessed human sacrifice, after great military victories when prisoners taken in battle were burned as a thanksgiving to the gods. The number sacrificed would depend on the importance of the battle, the size of the opposing force, and the rivalry between the tribe and its enemy. But such sacrifices were apparently offered only against those tribes which had themselves offered their enemies for human sacrifice after victories on the battlefield.

Following a triumphant victory against such an enemy, the Army of the Catuvellauni would build a colossal figure of a man out of tree branches and twigs which might be as much as 5m high. Those prisoners selected for the ritual sacrifice would be bound hand and foot and made to watch the building of the wooden figure. Then, one by one, the soldiers would push the prisoners through a hole in the 'neck' of the colossus until the entire figure was filled with the screaming victims.

Sometimes criminals, vagabonds and 'undesirables', as well as the captured warriors, would be offered to the gods as a thanksgiving for the great military victory. On such occasions, the tribe would gather at the place of sacrifice and cheer and scream their appreciation as the Catuvellauni soldiers stuffed the victims into the effigy before setting light to the pyre. They would cheer as they watched their enemies burn to death as the Druids in attendance offered thanks to the gods for the Army's victory. Sometimes, members of the tribe would dance around the effigy, praising the gods for delivering their enemies to their deaths.

If there were insufficient prisoners or criminals to hand, then innocent members of the tribe were offered to the gods in their place. These poor innocents would customarily be the old and the infirm, but youngsters who were in poor health would also be sacrificed.

Indeed, one of the harsh facts of life in pre-history Britain was the ruthless manner in which those who were of no further use to the tribe would simply be sacrificed to the gods in the belief that such a sacrifice would keep the remainder of the tribe healthy.[1]

Tasciovanus, and those who came before him, had been taught by the Druids that a man was a highly pleasing sacrifice to the gods. It had been the custom in earlier centuries that whenever a tribe settled in a new area, a human being would be sacrificed to purify the location. Both in Gaul and Britain, one of the poorest members of the tribe would be selected.

For exactly one year, the victim — which could be either a man or a woman — would be bestowed with privileges and persuaded to offer themselves as a human sacrifice. The 'volunteer' would be fed with choice food, provided with clothing and a round-house and, when the appointed day arrived, would be taken and offered in a ritual sacrifice, witnessed by the entire tribe. In Gaul, they would either stone the poor victim to death or throw him into the sea to drown. In ancient Britain, death by fire was the common practice.

In pre-history Britain, religious leaders had indulged in human sacrifices in their efforts to search for auguries of the future by examining the entrails of their victims. By the Year Zero, however, such indulgences had been abandoned.

The practice of these fortune-telling sacrifices would involve priests standing by and witnessing the hapless victim as he, or she, was held by both arms while a warrior repeatedly stabbed the person in the diaphragm, as the priest took note of the victim's convulsions. The priest would then examine in great detail whatever spewed from the wounds, making a careful and studied judgement. Then, as the wretched victim lay on the ground, blood oozing from the many stab wounds to his body, the Druid would make his pronouncements while members of the tribe looked on and waited with bated breath for his vision of the future. Afterwards, the poor victim would be killed, the body burned.

Tasciovanus himself frequently indulged in celebrations following famous military victories. When he did not personally participate in the battle, his soldiers would return bearing the severed heads of the enemy leaders which would be presented to him as trophies, as well as proof of their victory on the field of battle.

Sometimes, enemy leaders would be brought back to the tribal capital and, in full view of the assembled members of the tribe, including women and children, the enemy soldiers would be executed, their heads cut off with one stroke of a bronze axe. While the victorious tribal members cheered their approval, the head, still dripping blood, would be stuck on gates, fences or ramparts as a

---

[1] In his *Commentaries on the Gallic War* (Book VI, Chapter XIX), Caesar wrote that when a person of great importance in Britain died and was cremated, the mourners cast into the fire all things, including living creatures, which they supposed to have been dear to the dead man. Slaves and dependents who were ascertained to have been beloved by them were, after the regular funeral rites were completed, burnt together with them. It is not known how prevalent such human sacrifices were around the Year Zero but there seems proof enough that they did indeed take place.

warning to others that this tribe was ferocious and not to be challenged.

It often appeared to have the desired effect, frightening off potential attackers. An ancient Celtic belief was that the soul of a man reposed in the head, not in the heart, as Christianity believes. And that was the reason why the head was so venerated and prized in the ancient societies.

Certain ceremonial burnings and offerings took place at frequent intervals, usually when the Druids decided the time was ripe for a consecration or an offering to be made to the gods. Dogs, birds and sometimes even horses were burned and then the remains thrown in pits outside the perimeter of the village. These pits often took a great deal of hard work to be completed as they were sometimes the depth of three men.

Wild animals were not sacrificed to the gods because it was believed that a hunted beast would not be pleasing to the various deities. The entire ancient world practised ritual slaughter and animal sacrifice, and this was carried out at all levels of society not simply by the élite.

The ritual slaughter of animals represented not only the offering of wealth but also the most dramatic religious gesture known to man — the destruction of life. The drama was greatly increased if the victim was human. Caesar, Strabo and Diodorus all asserted that the tribes of Gaul and Britain ritually killed people as a sacrifice to the gods.

The Druids ordered the killing of captives taken in battle in order to discover the divine will in the flow of their blood or their palpitating entrails.

They administered to the sick and those going into battle who trusted that heaven would spare their lives if human victims were offered in their stead. And so criminals and vagabonds were sometimes ceremonially burned as an offering.

The Druids even countenanced the ritual slaughter of a child at the foundation of a monument, a fortress or a bridge to ensure the safety of all those who would in the future pass by the foundation stones.

Some tribes in pre-history Wales and Ireland allegedly offered a third of their healthy infants every year to the gods, apparently to ward off enemies and ensure that the tribe remained strong. But some historians believed this to be simply a fable.

Word of similar practices would have reached the ancient Britons about the events then taking place in Rome — in those days the capital of the known world. During the time of the late Republic and early Empire, the Romans would sacrifice their children in rites to conjure the spirits of the dead. The Romans, considered by many as the civilising influence of the world, frequently made human sacrifices both before and after battle to appease their gods.

Indeed, 100 years into the new millennium, Roman legions were still offering human sacrifices before going into battle. Apparently, the human sacrifices also took place after a major battle but these sacrifices took place whether the Roman legionnaires won or lost.

The merchants also recounted stories of human sacrifices that occurred in Greek civilisations. Greek literature provides evidence of human sacrificial customs including, in particular, the slaughter of young virgins before an important battle.

Within a century or so of the Year Zero, however, human sacrifices had all but ended, though the ritual sacrifice of animals would continue for centuries. These sacrifices and rituals were always performed with a Druid priest or priestess in attendance to make sure all was carried out correctly according to the unwritten traditions which had been passed down from generation to generation through the centuries.

The Roman legionnaires who later invaded Britain found the sacrifice of animals coincided with their own traditions, for the central feature of the public ceremonials in the official Roman religion was the sacrificing of animals at the altars of the gods. An official soothsayer — a position of great importance in the hierarchy of the Roman Empire — would then ceremonially inspect the entrails of the sacrificial animals in front of members of the Senate and others and would then make his pronouncements.

These judgements were treated with the greatest respect and many were acted upon. Weighty, vitally important decisions affecting the Roman Empire were made as a result of such pagan rituals. Upon such judgements, decisions would be taken as to whether Rome should send its legions to attack or conquer some region or country; the date and timing of such wars; even the numbers of legions required to undertake a particular venture would be decided. Such ceremonies would usually take place on the most important dates in Rome's religious calendar, especially when great matters of State were concerned.

Druids were forbidden by their religion to commit any of their traditions or teachings to the written word. As a result, those wishing to become Druids had to memorise a vast number of facts and verses, one of the reasons why those wishing to attain the highest form of Druidism took 20 years to complete their studies. The principal reason for this apparent necessity was the Druid's fear that if their doctrine, rituals and traditions were in written form they might become public knowledge and they were determined that the Druids should remain the élite of society, a privileged, almost secret sect.

Another reason was the fact that Druids believed that training the mind, and the memory, was the most important of all teachings and the written word made people less diligent in learning by heart.

One of the reasons for the enormous power and influence of the Druids was that they professed to know the will of the gods, meaning that the Druids believed they were the 'middle-men' and 'middle-women' between the mortal and immortal world. But that was only one of their functions. Indeed, many in ancient Britain believed that their gods were not simply creators but their ancestors, and they were therefore treated and respected more as supernatural heroes and heroines.

It had been during the lifetime of Tasciovanus's illustrious grandfather, King Cassivellaunus, that trade between ancient Britain and Gaul had increased dramatically, the principal reason being to re-supply the

Roman legions which had conquered and then occupied Gaul during that century. Vast amounts of wheat were needed to feed their armies, animal hides to cover their tents and wool for their clothing and blankets. And as that trade escalated, relations between the merchants and seafarers of ancient Britain, the people of Gaul and the Roman legions grew closer.

Tasciovanus would also have heard first hand about the violent, barbaric and bloodthirsty 'circuses' then taking place in Rome. From the fourth century BC onwards, the people of Rome flocked to see the savage spectacle of slaves and prisoners of war fighting to the death while the crowds in their thousands cheered and jeered. On other occasions, thousands of criminals were led into the arena in Rome and ritually slaughtered for the entertainment of the masses. These stories, all accurate, were brought back to Britain and spread throughout the land by word of mouth.

They told of hundreds of gladiators being assembled in the arena and then ordered to fight to the death until only one remained alive. In a single day, hundreds of criminals, both men and women, would be led in chains to the arena and wild animals, including half-starved lions and tigers, would be unleashed to kill and eat them while the spectators roared their approval. Slaughter by wild animals was found to be particularly appealing to the Roman masses. And the crowds roared their demands for their favourite special feature, the rape of young slave girls by wild beasts.

At the grand opening of the Colosseum, a total of 9,000 wild animals were recorded as being killed in fights with men and women. However, the number of men and women slaughtered that day was not recorded. But there is no suggestion whatsoever that such practices took place in ancient Britain.

The Druids were considered both the priestly class and the wise men of the tribe who carried on the traditions of those early Magi who had planned the stone circles of Britain, such as Stonehenge. The Druids continued the megalithic (stone worship) folk practices of ancient Neolithic (Stone Age) people certainly until the Year Zero and beyond. Tasciovanus was taught that the Druids' history went back many centuries and that Druids had once built temples to the god Apollo.

And yet the rites and teachings of Druidism seemed to have much in common with the religions of India, especially the similarities between the functions and the positions in society of the Druids and their Indian counterparts, the Brahmins, the wise men of the Hindu religion. Both Druid and Brahmin were heirs to a common tradition of learning and culture.

Among other similarities was the fact that some ancient British tribes fought naked in the belief that this would release their *karma* to its fullest potential, enhancing their capability throughout the battle and, if killed, would hasten their incarnation in the 'Otherworld'. The Hindu society of Kshatriya also held such a belief and practices.

Both the Hindus and the Druids worshipped sacred trees; Hindus considered the pipal, a large Indian fig tree, to be sacred, while the Druids took their name from the oak tree. The word Druid, as recognised by Greek writers, including Aristotle (384–322BC) meant 'those whose knowledge is great'.

Strabo and Pliny the Elder believed the word Druid came from the Greek *drus*, meaning 'an oak tree'. This is supported by many who believe Druid does indeed come from the Greek for oak, which in European history was associated with wisdom. Thus Druid culture is closely aligned with 'oak knowledge'.

The Druid caste had its roots in the earlier food-gathering age when extensive oak forests covered Europe. The oak was considered a symbol of plenty, providing acorns which were eaten in winter months, and which were sometimes ground and baked into bread. The early Europeans utilised oak wood for their fires and for their rough timber dwellings and the oak tree could be trusted to bear the hardiest and most useful wood.

As a result, over those thousand or more years, generations developed a veneration of the oak and gave rise to 'the wise ones of the oak', a central belief in many Indo–European religions. To have a knowledge of the trees endowed a person with survival techniques and, consequently, wisdom.

In ancient India, the agricultural tribes situated their villages near a sacred grove of trees or former forest reputed to be a remnant of the primeval forest left intact for the local gods when the land was cleared to ensure better agricultural use. Shiva, the great Hindu god, allegedly dwelt in a tree — the bel tree.

In ancient Briton, the great oak, the embodiment of a powerful, all-knowing god, became a religious symbol in various societies because of its majestic appearance, its size and its longevity compared with other trees. It was also an ancient phallic symbol. Across Europe, many societies worshipped the powers of the oak; some associated it with the god of thunder, while others ritually sacrificed an oak tree by burning it to ashes, in the belief that it would produce good crops.

The Druids' sacred tree was a rowan — a mountain ash. At night, some Druids would lie on the wattle of this tree to stimulate prophetic visions. The hazel tree was also important because it was believed that the hazelnuts held a nucleus of wisdom.

In the centuries around 4,000BC, Europe was covered with oak forests, and primitive hunter-gatherers saw the oak as a symbol of plenty, a tree from which they would collect acorns as an integral part of their staple diet. Easy to store and carry, easy to grind and bake into bread, the acorn was a life-preserver to many ancient tribes.

Oak was also respected as the tree that supplied excellent hard wood for burning, as well as being used to build timber dwellings to shelter families. Early Europeans venerated the oak as the greatest tree of the forest, the hardiest and most useful which would grow and mature for hundreds of years. Some believed it might never die if not cut down.

As a result, the veneration of the oak, and the rise of the wise ones of the oak, became a central belief in most ancient Indo–European religions.

In the Hindu religion, for example, the pipal tree — the large Indian fig tree — was considered sacred for that tree was, allegedly, the one chosen by the god Brahma — the supreme Hindu deity — to inhabit with Vishnu, another supreme god, making their home in the twigs. Indeed, each leaf was dutifully assigned to one of the deities.

By the start of the first millennium BC, when the Celts began to journey far and wide, all learned men and women were designated as having 'oak knowledge'. And, in the Celtic religion itself, the oak continued to be venerated as the great symbol of natural abundance so that, as a cult, its symbolism was retained among the Celts for many centuries.

Most hamlets and villages in pre-history Britain were selected and built around a tree which immediately took on a sacred status. It was usually called the tree of life, standing as a talisman in the centre of the community. Sometimes, raiding parties would attack a small commune solely with the intent of cutting down the sacred tree to shatter the spirit of the villagers.

These attacks would often have such a profound effect on the settlement that the village leaders would decide to move the entire settlement and all their animals to another site and set up a new hamlet around another tree they deemed to be sacred. A successful attack against a settlement would frequently undermine the chieftain, making him appear to the villagers to be a weak leader, incapable of defending his people.

As a result of felling the sacred tree of a village, some marauding warriors would decide to stay in their newly conquered settlement. They believed they had won the right to move in and keep the cattle and other animals as well as any of the village women they wanted. Young, strong men who had been captured might also be taken to be used or sold as slaves.

Some nations, including those of Slavic and German origin, believed the oak tree was associated with their respective god of thunder, and some Asiatic tribes believed that when they died their souls would take up residence in such trees. And even the more 'sophisticated' people of Greece and Rome once shared the oak cult.

Zeus was once worshipped in the oracular oak at Dodona.[1] Jupiter, the Roman equivalent of Zeus, was worshipped on the Capitol where a sacred oak tree stood. The Temple of Vesta — goddess of hearth and household — in the Forum had fires which had to be fuelled by oak and no other wood. In the hope of raising good crops, villages sometimes 'sacrificed' an oak tree by ritual burning, while other tribes would smear the blood of sacrificial animals on oak trees in the belief that this would guarantee rain and a good harvest.

Although the oak was seen as the ultimate phallic symbol and most of the oak adoration and worship in many societies centred around its masculine connotations, the Celts started with a mother goddess concept. Most religions of the world include a 'mother goddess' figure, as did the ancient British. In the case of the Celts, the mother goddess was called Danu, and in Sanskrit the word Dana means 'waters of heaven'. That same name also forms the root of one of the the great European rivers, the Danube, at whose headwaters Celtic civilisation is acknowledged to have evolved. Indeed, the region of the headwaters of the Upper Danube, the Rhone and the Rhine, with all their tributaries, is a region full of Celtic names.

The names of such rivers in Britain such as the Severn, the Dee, the Clyde and the Brent, as well as the River Boyne in Ireland, all reflect the same association of a river with a goddess. It was deemed that the main river — the mother-river — watered a whole region, just as in Hindu culture the waters are revered as mothers, sources of fertility. The Celts regarded rivers as bestowers of life, health and plenty and, on occasions, they would offer the waters rich gifts and sacrifices.

The Druids believed that water symbolised the female element of life while the oak became the male symbol and, as a symbol of natural abundance, water was accepted as a fertility symbol. The belief was that water, in the form of the mother goddess, nourished the oak and gave it birth. Many of the deities of pre-history Britain were associated with water and, particularly, springs. Ritual pits and shafts were dug and often dedicated to a local god or a spirit and locally made artefacts were dropped into the well as an offering.

Despite centuries of Christian misinformation and corrupt teaching to denigrate Druids as barbaric priests or priestesses, they were respected intellectuals who had appeared in other guises in most other civilisations within Europe, Egypt, Spain and north Africa. They formed the intelligentsia, or learned class and were deemed the highest

---

[1] Tacitus (55-120AD), the great Roman historian who married the daughter of the Emperor Agricola, wrote of the greatest shrines of the classical world being revered features, such as trees or rocks, and usually situated in rural and often extremely remote areas in forests and mountains.

caste. And though they had a priestly function, they were not solely priests.

The Druids were a caste incorporating all the learned professions. Some were philosophers, others judges, teachers, historians, poets, musicians, physicians, astronomers, prophets and, importantly, political advisers.

They formed an unofficial type of secret society, admission to which was eagerly sought by many fathers for their sons and, to a lesser extent, their daughters. They were ruled by a pope who held office for life, but their doctrine and lore were a closely guarded secret. Sometimes, the succession to the position of pope was so ferociously disputed that war lords were called in to settle the matter by force of arms.

They held, as the priests of any such society always have, a monopoly over learning. The ignorance and superstition of the people, their own organisation and submission to a pope, gave the religious leaders tremendous power. The doctrine, which they most strenuously insisted upon, was the transmigration of souls. This doctrine was at the forefront of the Druids' teachings, regarded as the most potent incentive to valour, inspiring a contempt for death.

Though the Druids preached the doctrine of transmigration of the soul, it was not accepted by the mass of the British people who, in Year Zero, still held firm in the belief that there was a future life after death, a form of the 'Continuance Theory' which for centuries held sway in primitive and more modern tribes. The Britons believed that there was an abode of the blessed, a place of perfect happiness, somewhere where they would live again, feasting, carousing and enjoying a blissful existence.

The power and influence of the Druids came as no surprise to the invading Romans for, only decades earlier, the Romans occupying Gaul had become so fearful of their power they had taken ruthless steps to drive them from the country. To Rome, the Druids represented an intellectual and challenging opposition. The Romans were materialistic, the Druids spiritual.

Romans demanded their State be a monolithic structure spread across the western world; in contrast, the Druids wanted a freely consented moral order. Rome based its law on private ownership of land with property rights entirely vested in the head of the family. Druids always considered ownership to be collective.

As a result, the Romans came to fear societies in which the Druids were respected and, as was the way with the authoritarian Roman élite, they wanted to suppress them, fearful that what they saw as the Druids' subversive ideas would threaten the ordered Roman world. Indeed, one of the reasons Julius Caesar decided to invade Britain was because he feared the Druid influence might gain a greater foothold in Gaul and become a more dynamic subversive influence in that recently conquered country.

Another reason for the Roman fear of Druid influence was the Druidic attitude to women. Romans looked upon women as bearers of children and objects of pleasure to be used and abused as men saw fit, while the Druids respected women, including them in both their political and religious life. Indeed, in some societies in which Druids held sway, women were sometimes elected as chiefs and had the same rights as all the men of the tribe. And we have noted, on occasions through history, female figures held supreme command, such as Boadicea in AD61 and Cartismandua from AD43–69.

In ancient Greece, women had no political rights and even their social rights were limited.

They could not own or inherit property or enter into business or barter transactions. Indeed, Greek women were accepted as an inheritable chattel, and were restricted as to where they were allowed to walk or roam or where they could visit.

In Rome, women did enjoy more rights and could visit shops, theatres and other public places as long as they were respectably clothed, though the man of the house, either a father or husband, still had complete control over his female charges.

At that same time in history, when most societies treated women as mere chattels, in Ireland and some parts of Britain women became lawyers and judges. They could also inherit and own property and women remained the owner of any property brought into a marriage. If the marriage broke up, the woman not only kept all her own property but also any gifts given to her by her husband during the marriage. A woman was also solely responsible for her own debts and not those of her husband. But, of course, very few women in pre-history Britain ever married, they simply lived with a number of men; the rite of marriage was reserved only for the nobility, the powerful and the wealthy.

In principle, women could not only become Druids

but were accepted, like men, as prophets, bards, doctors and even satirists. Some female Druids practised witchcraft and indulged in magic while other female Druids served a deity resembling Bacchus, the god of wine and ecstasy. There also existed a community of Druid women who allegedly could raise storms, cause diseases and kill their enemies simply by the use of supernatural curses.

One such Druidess in Celtic mythology was a young priestess named Fidelma[1] who claimed she could prophesy the future. She was described as follows:

> 'She had yellow hair. She wore a speckled cloak fastened around her with a gold pin, a red embroidered hooded tunic and sandals with gold clasps. Her brow was broad, her jaw narrow, her two eyebrows pitch black, with delicate dark lashes casting shadows halfway down her cheeks. You could think her lips were inset with Parthian scarlet. Her teeth were like an array of jewels between the lips. She had hair in three tresses; two would upward on her head and the third hung down her back, brushing her calves. She held a light weaving rod in her hand, with gold inlay. Her eyes had triple irises. Two black horses drew her chariot, and she was armed.'

Such fanciful descriptions of young women reveal what writers in early Britain believed was the epitome of beauty. Before many decades into the new millennium, however, the male-dominated Christian religion was gaining ground and, backed by the male chauvinists of Rome, the attitude to women was to change dramatically.

Over time, the female Druids were relegated to 'fairy women' or 'witches' and the concept of a Druidess changed to that of a sorceress, an enchantress, a hell-cat. In this way, the Christian church was able to describe such women as representing paganism, which the early Christians were keen to portray as heathen, unenlightened, irreligious and damned in the eyes of God.

But it was the sun that Tasciovanus, the Catuvellauni tribe and most other tribes dutifully worshipped. It didn't matter how many other gods or deities people from different tribes honoured, venerated or entreated, for the great majority of ancient Britons worshipped the sun. Indeed, people in the hundreds of tribes and communities throughout Britain worshipped many different gods and deities in those days of pre-history.

Figures of deities were usually carved out of wood, the females carved with a large hole in the centre of the body, the men portrayed with a large phallus plugged into the hole. There were neither breasts nor rounded hips on the female bodies so that both figures could be used for male or female deities saving time, energy and the complication of having to carve separate wooden bodies.

In some hamlets and villages, there were also human images carved out of stone and huge boulders and these, too, were venerated as local gods. Indeed, some societies worshipped large stones and boulders on which nothing had been carved at all. Sometimes, large stones became objects of worship locally, perhaps because of something as

---

[1] In the most famous epic of Irish mythology, *The Cattle Raid of Cuailnge*, the Queen of Connach consults the young Druidess named Fidelma. The exact date of the epic is not known, although the first reference to it is in 7AD.

banal as the sun shining on them in some unusual way, bestowing them with a mysterious air, affording the rock the status of an object to be revered, an idol. Many such local gods were given no names but the place or the object was simply referred to as 'the spirit of the place'.

But it was the life-giving sun that was always revered. Centuries before, the ancient men and women who peopled Britain had learned that the worship of the sun in ancient Egypt had existed since the beginning of time, although other Gods had sometimes grown in importance, had won devotees and had been glorified and honoured. At the same time, however, the people had continued to worship the sun above all other deities and idols.

Ancient Britons, whose inhabitants arrived in the islands from the Middle East and from eastern and western Europe over many, many centuries, had erected altars as other civilisations had done for a great variety of reasons. The idea of erecting altars to various gods had been imported into Britain and tribes had found in this act of devotion and dedication a central focus for their village, hamlet, community or tribe. On the majority of these altars the solar symbol — the six-spoked solar wheel — was carved.

The sun was worshipped simply because it brought forth the harvest producing the food that sustained all life. It was recognised that without sun nothing would grow or could grow and therefore nothing could live or even survive. The sun was seen as omnipotent, the very essence of life without which everyone and everything would die.

Many other gods were honoured and revered for a

hundred and one different reasons by the various tribes throughout the land, but the sun was always the ultimate god, the life-bearer, the life-giver. Historians have since suggested that they have traced nearly 400 names of Celtic gods and goddesses throughout Europe in areas which Celts once inhabited. But there were likely to have been hundreds more. Nothing had altered that state of affairs since worship began.

That didn't deter some tribes from taking great pains to carve and erect images of their own gods and idols. Some tribes, particularly those which were having success on the field of battle, would carve human images which were meant to be the likeness of the local chief or the tribe's most famous warrior. The carvings, nearly always in rock or stone, were quite rudimentary, but some carvings would take a gifted stone mason months to complete to his satisfaction. Indeed, it should be recognised that some of the images of humans were beautifully and skilfully carved, despite the fact that the mason had only the most basic and crude implements at his disposal.

Understandably, many of these human carvings were phallic symbols, carved as a supplication to the gods, praying that the village women would produce many healthy babies to ensure the future of the tribe. Such ritualistic homage was treated as a vitally important necessity by the elders of the tribe when many of their young men were so frequently killed in battle.

Other human carvings, usually boasting phallic symbols, were adored because the statue was meant to be a likeness of the local chieftain. In many tribes, the chief would take his pick of the young women, as many as he wanted, to be used not merely as objects of pleasure but, far more importantly, as a means of ensuring the tribe's future.

Understandably, in such societies the mothers of the young women, the majority as young as 12 and 13 years of age, would consider it a privilege if one of their offspring was selected by the chief to bear his child. Of course, the mother-to-be had no say whatsoever in whether they were offered to the local chief as child-bearers.

For the same reason — the all-important necessity of ensuring the continuance of the human species — there was one particular idol that was frequently carved throughout ancient Britain, as it was in civilisations across the known world, and that was of the mother-goddess or earth-mother. In Britain's pre-history these carvings, both rudimentary and obvious, frequently showed a woman with a large head and protruding eyes with her legs wide apart and her hands frozen in the act of opening her huge vagina as though about to give birth.

In the great majority of villages which boasted a number of round-houses, there were usually altars built of wood and these, too, were decorated with carvings. Surprisingly, no altars were built of rock or stone but the carvings found on the wooden altars was evidence of which gods that particular community worshipped. Many sported the sun-god but the great majority depicted gods which later generations found impossible to identify.

Despite the enormous number of different gods worshipped by the many British tribes, it appeared that no one gave names to these gods. Of course, no one in ancient

Britain ever wrote down anything before the Roman invasion, let alone the names of local gods and, as a result, no names of these local gods are known.

Indeed, after the Roman invasion, it appears that for decades, and for centuries in Wales and Scotland, many tribes took not the slightest notice of the gods the Romans brought to Britain, preferring to continue worshipping their local gods and, of course, the sun. It seems that many tribes were determined to keep their old traditions secret, worshipping their own gods, deities and idols and keeping such worship to themselves away from the prying eyes of the Roman Army.

Some tribes even revered animals, particularly horses, and these were quite often erected as idols and carved from stone to stand in the midst of the local community as some sort of symbol marking out the animal as an idol to be honoured.

When Caesar visited Britain during his two invasions, he recorded that the tribesmen of Britain worshipped Mercury, Apollo, Mars and, first and foremost, Jupiter, the sun-god, just as the people of Gaul did at that time. It was only after Rome's successful invasion of Britain in AD43 that the truth of the facts of pagan religion and the multitude of different gods gradually emerged.

Religious buildings were constructed on the edge of large villages in which the inhabitants would go to pray to their gods. Some holy buildings could hold as many as 50 people while others could hold perhaps a dozen or so. There were other, private places which would accommodate only one person. The doors of nearly all these buildings faced towards the sun rise, north-east to south-east. Some were sited in their own enclosures, but all were separate from the rest of the village.

Some such buildings were some distance away from the main village, reached only by a special journey and known only to those who worshipped there. Inside, the believers would leave presents to the gods such as weapons, animal bones, brooches and jewellery, coins, pots and horse harnesses. Offerings of food, drink or cloth were also made. Some tribes preferred to worship in open spaces near groves and by mountains, rivers and springs.

The intellectual élite were divided into Bards, Druids and Vates, the last two categories being religious officials. The Druids were considered the more prestigious, occupying themselves with philosophy and theology, while the Vates were concerned with divination and sacrifice. Sometimes the Druids undertook the task of the Vates. Bards, who were apparently Druids of an inferior grade, sat at the tables of the great and the nobility, some accompanied them with their harps at festivals, sang their praises, satirised their enemies and recited poems in honour of valiant warriors who had fallen in battle.

Druids were also teachers, healers and judges, physicians and historians, astronomers and astrologers, seers and magicians, poets and musicians. And they kept the all-important calendar around which ancient society was organised.

In Year Zero, the Druids of Britain used the Coligny calendar which had been skilfully prepared 100 years earlier. It seems to have been based on the Hindu calendar.

The Coligny calendar, though, is based on a five-year synchronisation of the lunar and solar year, a masterpiece of calculation and proof of the Druids' astronomical brilliance. The calendar consisted of 62 consecutive months, divided into a period of 29 or 30 nights each. At the end of a three-year cycle, an extra month was added. The Druids used nights because they believed it more accurate to measure their months and years by the moon rather than the sun. The Coligny calendar was indeed more elaborate than the Julian calendar but just as accurate.

For centuries, Stonehenge has intrigued and baffled archaeologists, historians, mathematicians and astronomers. However, with the help of modern computers and scientific techniques, it now seems almost certain that not only was Stonehenge constructed with the numbers indicated in the Coligny calendar, but that, more than likely, it was the earliest Druids who were responsible for what has been described as an 'astronomical computer'. And construction began in the second Millennium BC, around 4,000 years ago!

To have accomplished such a sensational construction, the Druids must have had a profound knowledge of prehistoric astronomy and amazing mathematical skill. It is now accepted that Stonehenge stands in the best possible position for observing the heavenly bodies, as there is a horizon nearly three miles distant on all sides. It is also a fact that the principal axis was aligned to the midsummer sunrise.

Despite modern computers and all the technology of the twenty-first century, however, no one has been yet able to explain satisfactorily the theoretical use of Stonehenge. The most likely explanation was that Stonehenge was constructed as a huge, and amazingly accurate, astronomical instrument.

And the Druid's fascination and interest in astronomy and astrology continued for centuries. Caesar, Strabo, Cicero, Pliny and other classical writers paid tribute to the Druids' understanding of the stars as well as their 'speculation by the stars'. These ancient writers accepted that the Druids 'knew the shape and size of the world, the movements of the heavens and of the stars'.[1]

It was, indeed, not until the eighteenth century, during the so-called 'Age of Reason', that astronomy and astrology were separated and became two distinct sciences. Historians of astrology believe its origins came from Babylon and made its way to Greece, and many quote Aristotle constantly using the word rather than 'astronomy' which he, in fact, studied. From the beginning of the human species, it was believed by most societies across the world that the stars influenced individuals and events on earth. Those societies noticed that the sun and the moon affected the tides, that the sun regulated the seasons and they also believed that the moon could affect the behaviour of men and women.

As well as being astronomers and astrologers, Druid priests also cared for holy shrines and were responsible for supervising sacrifices, making prophecies, healing the sick, teaching the privileged and giving sound counsel.

It was as judges that Druids were also held in the highest regard. It was Caesar and also Strabo who wrote that the judges in ancient Britain were always Druids and both men seemed to have a high opinion of the Druids' capability and objectivity. Indeed, Druids were entrusted with all the legal decisions taken by the various tribes, and also individuals, though there were, seemingly, no written laws for them to refer to.

Once again, it reveals the extraordinary trust that all tribal leaders, both friends and foes, had placed in the Druids. Importantly, there was no appeal to a higher authority permitted after a decision had been reached by Druid judges for they were considered pre-eminent in all legal matters.

Some Druids were also held in high regard for their medical knowledge. In the half century before Year Zero, Pliny confirmed their capability, writing that the Druids' ability was so well renowned that Roman physicians were sent to study under them and learn from their expertise and knowledge. In those days of ancient history, medicine and astrology were closely combined, particularly in the diagnosis of people's illnesses and complaints. Indeed, in his *Natural History*, Pliny wrote that he believed the historical basis for the power and influence of Druids derived principally from their medico-magical knowledge.

Both male and female Druids were respected as surgeons and healers, as well as being skilled in herbal preparations for dealing with most ailments. What is extraordinary 2,000 years on is that Druids performed some remarkable, daring and quite exceptional major

[1] The historian Pomponius Mela (10-75AD) wrote in high regard of the Druids claiming they also knew the movements of tides through the actions of the moon and of the cause of the midnight sun.

surgical operations including births by Caesarean section, amputations and brain surgery.[1] Many appear to have been successful.

It is not known what herbal drugs, or alcohol, if either, were used during such operations, but it is known that the first histroical use of drugs connected with surgical operations did take place in Egypt three centuries before Year Zero. That was about 100 years after the famous Greek physician Hippocrates (460BC–370BC) from the tiny island of Kos wrote his famous *Oath* which is honoured in modern medicine to this day.

It seems extraordinary that at Year Zero in pre-history Britain, which writers and historians have suggested was a barbaric country on the edge of the known world, was, in fact, peopled by at least one section of society, the Druids, who were a highly intelligent, well-educated, multi-talented and reasonable group capable of running society on many different levels.

The power of the Druids seemed to know no bounds. Druids were even permitted and, on occasions, actively encouraged, to intervene on the field of battle and stop opposing armies fighting. Tasciovanus had witnessed such an action when his tribe was involved in inter-tribal warfare against a weaker opponent. And the Roman writer Diodorus Siculus supports this extraordinary power which the Druids held by right.

He wrote, 'Often when the combatants are ranged face to face, and swords drawn and spears bristling, these men come between the armies and stay the battle, just as wild beasts are sometimes held spellbound.'

This was also confirmed by Strabo, who wrote, 'Druids even arbitrated in cases of war and made the opponents stop when they were about to line up for battle.'

The Druids saw a person's life divided into two halves of three periods each. The first part was infancy, the second childhood and the third puberty. In the second half was manhood, old age and finally senility. The Druids also held elaborate rituals for the funerals. These funerals were a celebration, a rebirth of the dead person in the next world. The deceased would be ceremonially washed and then wrapped in a clean shroud. Depending on his or her importance, Druids would watch over the body, and in the case of a king or chieftain, for perhaps 12 days and nights. The body was then placed on a bier and then lowered into a grave while requiems were sung by those who had gathered around the grave.

In earlier times, before the Roman invasions, bodies of chiefs were usually cremated and, at the same time, all the prisoners held by the chief at that time were also ceremonially burned along with all his favourite animals, such as horses or dogs. This custom of course was closely related to the Indian custom of *sati* (from the Sanskrit meaning 'devoted wife') in which the widow followed her husband on to the funeral pyre. Sometimes, a warrior was buried standing upright with his weapons.

[1] In January 1935, a fisherman trawling off the coast of Ovingdean in Sussex collected a skull in his nets. It was later dated by experts to the pre-Christian Celtic period. The skull had two large round holes deliberately cut into it over the brain. The ancient surgeons had cut into this person on two separate occasions, the healing of the bone around both holes indicating that the patient survived the operation but eventually died of sepsis some weeks after the second operation. To perform a trephining operation with the patient surviving indicates a very advanced degree of medical knowledge and the evidence that it occurred is in keeping with the reports of Pliny the Elder (AD23–AD79), who praised the Druids for their medical knowledge.

Ancient Britons believed the soul survived death. Caesar and Pomponius were reminded of the Greek doctrine of Pythagoras whereby souls were reborn in new bodies. But some Britons believed that human beings transcended the grave.

Some tribes would burn or bury the favourite possessions of the deceased so that the gods could accompany him or her into the new life, a place they called the 'Otherworld'. They believed there was 'another supernatural world' where people enjoyed eternal life in the sense that they did not grow old or fall sick, yet they could, apparently, be killed. What happened to their spirits in that event was never explained.

The Otherworld could be entered from the earthly world by certain secret doors concealed in mounds, hills or in the floors of lakes or seas. Some special humans, like royalty or heroes, could apparently penetrate it and return to earth as humans, a sort of transmigration of souls to new bodies, a belief which was accepted in some parts of the ancient world from Egypt to China.

Druids also became involved in some rather bizarre, unusual or simply odd rituals, by our standards. One such ritual was the cutting of mistletoe which was accompanied by the sacrifice of two white bulls. The Romans also used to sacrifice two white oxen to the god Jupiter at the Capitol in Rome. In the Celtic language, then the principal spoken word in ancient Britain, mistletoe meant 'all healing'. It was a Druidic belief that when mistletoe is taken in a drink, it imparts fertility to barren animals and is an antidote to all poisons. In herbal traditions, however, mistletoe is accepted as a relief for nervous disorders, as well as being a narcotic. Apparently, the Druids would don a white tunic for the mistletoe cutting ceremony.

The driving of cattle past fire was a rite which the Druids monitored. It was accepted as a solemn, religious observation, which took place every year. The perceived wisdom was that such a ritual protected the cattle from disease. Two Druids would cast various spells over the cattle which were then driven between the two officiants and past the fire.

Festivals were a frequent event in the life of the Druid community. Dates of the festivals would be announced by the Druids who would call together all members of the tribe. They would also have the power and authority to summon rulers and chiefs to a festival where warriors would show off their skills in front of the villagers, demonstrating their ability to stand fast against attackers.

Warriors would make outrageous, self-important boasts and issue challenges to others. These challenges would, more often than not, be taken up by other warriors and the villagers would be treated to mock fights between various combatants. Usually, these contests were nothing more than feats of strength but they did provide some sport which provided the villagers with a break from their hard life of tiresome, tedious, never-ending labour.

More important, however, were the tribal feasts which were a great source of revelry when everyone would let their hair down and enjoy the merry-making, including the women and children. Calves or deer would be slaughtered, roasted on a spit and the entire village would join in the feasting. During the feast held on 1 November, a goat was sacrificed in the belief this would ensure there would be enough food for the tribe to last throughout the cold winter months ahead.

These feasts were held on the four most important dates of the ancient calendar[1] — 1 May, 1 August, 1 November and 1 February. May was by far and away the most important date because that was the first day of the New Year, a time for celebration after months of freezing cold winter frosts, snow, sleet and storms. Spring, when trees came into leaf, flowers bloomed, crops were sown, birds eggs hatched and the sun warmed the land again, was accepted as the start of the year, the beginning of new life.

Julius Caesar was the man responsible for providing the information which scholars relied on for centuries in their efforts to learn about and understand the mysterious Druids in letters he wrote back home to Rome. Caesar wrote of the length of study involved in becoming a Druid which, he claimed, was sometimes 20 years. He suggested there were great schools of Druidic learning in Britain and others wrote of Druids teaching their pupils in secret either in caves, secluded valleys or dark forests.

But Caesar, along with many other Greek and Roman classic writers, didn't refer to Druids as priests, claiming they were philosophers. In Gaul at this time some Druids — the teachers — certainly spent most of their lives with young male and female students teaching them all they knew about the world, the human soul and the gods.

Others contended that young boys and girls didn't attend a single place for their schooling but that Druids roamed the countryside lecturing privileged youngsters wherever they went, passing on their knowledge. And because Druid priests were always shown great respect, they were offered gifts of food and shelter by the head of the tribes or village whenever they visited.

The philosophy of the Druids was summed up by Diodorus Siculus, the Roman writer: 'The Druid joined to the study of nature that of moral philosophy, asserting that the human soul is indestructible, and also the universe, but that some time or other, fire and water will prevail.'

Another ancient writer, Diogenes Laertius, believed that the Druids' main principle was that the people 'should worship the gods, do no evil and exercise courage'. Their fundamental faith seemed to be that the Druids believed that man should live in harmony with nature, accepting that pain and death were not evils but part of the divine plan and that the only evil was moral weakness. Truth, above all else, was the paramount virtue.

And truth was not only the philosophical preserve of the Druids but also the basic Indo–European idea that truth is synonymous with divinity. Both the Druids and Indian Brahmins believed that truth was the ultimate cause of all being and that by means of truth the earth endures. The Druids and Brahmins proclaimed the myth that retribution

---

[1] These dates are extrapolated from the ancient Coligny calendar, details of which were found at Coligny in the department of the Ain in France. This calendar, engraved in bronze, which was discovered in 1890, had its lucky and unlucky days. Certain days would be regarded as suitable for sacrifices as well as for other functions. The Roman calendar, which, of course, pre-dated the Julian calendar — named after Julius Caesar — was often in disagreement with the Julian calendar. In Smith's *Dictionary of Greek and Roman Antiquities* (circa 1900), the writers affirm, 'it is very difficult or rather quite impossible to determine the actual dates in pre-history to correspond to the nominal dates of any events before the Julian reform of the calendar.'

followed a person who did not speak the truth. They maintained that whenever people did not tell the truth, marks would appear on their skin so the world would know they were lying. The most famous modern survival of that ancient myth is the tale of Pinocchio, the Italian story depicting the little boy whose nose grew longer every time he told a lie.

It was not only the common man who had to submit to the power of the Druids, for their writ also included authority over kings and tribal chiefs. Around the time of Year Zero, the word of the Druids in Gaul, Britain, Ireland and Galatia (Turkey) was treated with great esteem, even reverence, and was always obeyed, placing them in a position of great power and influence.

Druids not only had power of authority over kings and tribal chiefs but, in many cases, this was construed to mean that no major decision could be taken even by a king without first being given permission to follow a certain course of action. A noted Roman historian, Dio Chrysostom — known as Chrysostomos, meaning golden mouthed — wrote of the Druids in his famous *Oratio*, that, like the Brahmins of India, they held great political influence in Celtic society and were credited with remarkable intellectual attainments and wisdom.

He also wrote, 'The Celts appointed Druids, who were versed in the art of seers and other forms of wisdom, without whom the kings were not permitted to adopt or plan any course, so that, in fact, it was these who ruled and the kings became their subordinates and instruments of their judgement, while themselves seated on golden thrones and dwelling in great houses and being sumptuously feasted.'

During the last 2,000 years, however, respect for the mighty Druids has been slowly, continually and deliberately undermined principally by the forces of the Christian church. For centuries now, Druids have been dismissed as mere magicians, wizards in pointed black hats, wearing beards and walking around in long white robes chanting incantations to pagan gods and waving magic wands.

Originally, the Magi were the wise men and priestly caste of ancient Persia and their alleged powers over the supernatural gave us the word magic. In essence, the Magi were the equivalent of the Druids of Europe. After the Romanisation of Britain in the first four centuries following the birth of Jesus, there was abundant evidence of magic in myths and sagas suggesting that the Druids controlled the forces of nature by sorcery. In essence, this was no different from the earlier cultures of Rome and Athens in which the casting of spells, charms and curses were believed to affect, influence and control the course of human events.

The demise of the Druids began in Gaul where the Roman Emperor Claudius, who reigned from AD41 and died under suspicious circumstances in AD54, followed the earlier lead of the Emperor Tiberius, who not only excluded Druids from Roman citizenship by a decree of the Roman Senate but ordered the Druids' total extermination throughout Gaul. All this took place in the 50 years following Year Zero.

The Romans first ruthlessly suppressed Druidism in

Gaul and then did so in Britain but, apparently, without quite so much violence. The Romans were determined to wipe out any opposition to the authoritarian rule of the Roman Empire and, understandably, feared an intellectual class which had such power throughout the land in every facet of life, particularly political power and influence.

Destroying the opposition had always been the Roman way of dealing with political or social issues and through the centuries had become a highly successful method of maintaining the Empire's power and influence as well as forcing all alternative philosophies to obey the will of Rome or take the consequences. And the consequences were dire. So many kings, tribal chiefs, war lords and men of influence throughout Europe had been hauled back to Rome, sometimes put on trial and then dealt with brutally.

Those who had dared to challenge the Roman legions were dragged through the streets of Rome, chained to the chariots of victorious generals and ritually strangled in the Tullianum at the foot of the Capitol to appease Mars, the Roman god of war. Other leaders were thrown to the lions at the Roman circuses while the thousands in attendance cheered and jeered the unfortunate victims.

The Druids of Gaul and Britain understood the Roman determination and ruthless tactics and reacted in two different ways after the tribal armies of ancient Britain had been put to the sword by the mighty Roman legions.

Many Druids melted into the background, seeking refuge in forests and living as far away as possible from the clutches of the Roman conquerors. Many moved away from the south and east of Britain to Ireland, Wales and north of the Pennines where they continued their way of life for decades. Some continued teaching the young in secret, passing on their wisdom as they had always done. Eventually, however, the Druids realised that the power of Rome was too great and all-pervading to challenge directly and, over the years, many adopted the new religion of Christianity, some even becoming priests and continuing as a teaching and intellectual class in much the same way as the Druids had for centuries.

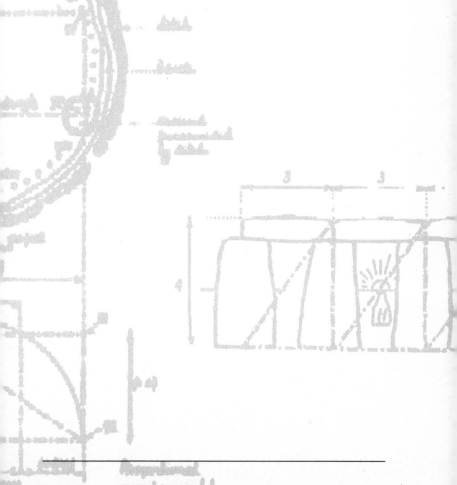

5.

INVASION

'I came, I saw, I conquered' ('Veni, vidi, vici' as Julius Caesar wrote in his famous commentaries on the war against Britain). Those three words, which so brilliantly and so succinctly encapsulated Caesar's successful invasion of Britain, made his campaign appear more like a walk in the park than a fiercely fought series of battles against courageous, daring and highly effective warriors.

Britain's tribal leaders were fortunate that they were not taken unawares. They knew the famous Roman general, whose reputation was feared by tribes throughout Europe and the Middle East, was about to lead an invasion of their island probably some six months or more before Caesar actually set sail from Gaul.

Gaius Julius Caesar, born in 100BC and assassinated in 44BC, was not only a famous general but also a statesman of repute from an ancient patrician family. Most of his illustrious life was spent on the battlefield and yet he began his career as a sea captain leading a small naval force against a host of pirates when aged 25. A succession of daring victories at sea propelled him into becoming an instant Roman hero and, in 73BC, he was elected to the privileged position of a *pontifex*, a member of the principal college of priests in ancient Rome. It was only the start of an illustrious career as one of the Roman Empire's greatest leaders. For most of the following 30 years, however, Caesar spent most of his life moving from Europe to Italy to Egypt, engaging in major wars against many of Rome's most audacious enemies and rebellious tribes.

But Caesar's brilliance and his reputation came to a high point during the last six years of his extraordinary life when civil war broke out in Rome with the Roman senate, led by Gnaeus Magnus Pompey (106BC-46BC), moving against Caesar. Pompey, to whom Caesar had given his daughter Julia in marriage, was jealous of his father-in-law and was determined to usurp his position. If that meant crushing the great general on the field of battle then so be it. In the end, Caesar's crack legionaries, who trusted implicitly in their military leader, defeated Pompey's much larger armies. Weeks after an emphatic defeat, Pompey was murdered after fleeing to a self-imposed exile in Egypt. Caesar was now the undisputed hero of Rome and the senate hailed him. His reward was to be appointed 'Dictator for Life' by the Roman Senate and received the title of 'Father of His Country'. Caesar's 'person' was even declared sacred, his statue placed in temples, his portrait struck on coins and the month of Quintilis renamed Julius (July) in his honour. But conspirators, mainly aristocrats jealous of Caesar's authority and autocratic powers, moved against him, ostensibly to restore political freedom to the Republic. And, of course, he was famously assassinated on the Ides (15th) of March in 44BC.

And this was the man who, at the height of his military career, decided to invade Britain and bring the islands under the control and influence of the Roman Empire. Despite the detail of his famous commentaries, written in the third person, Caesar never suggested the reason why he chose to conquer Britain. And no one had any idea for how long he had been shaping the project in his mind before he set about putting it into operation.

Perhaps the only clue to his reason for the invasion lies in the remark that, in almost all his Gallic campaigns, contingents of warriors from Britain had been fighting on the side of his enemies. In other passages, he testified to the close connections between Britain and Gaul, noting that on some occasions defeated chieftains would flee the continent and take refuge with a friendly tribe in Britain. Caesar also believed that a small number of chieftains held power both in Gaul and Britain.

The more rebellions that took place in western Europe, in areas which Caesar and his legions had already conquered, the more Caesar became preoccupied with the problem of keeping the peace among the fiercely independent tribes he had defeated on the field of battle. It is believed that the principal reason for his decision to invade the British Isles, which educated Romans believed were covered in rain and mist and were at the outer edge of the known world, was his determination to stamp out rebellion. It had taken Caesar little over three years, with the assistance of only six legions, to overrun the whole of Gaul and reach the Bay of Biscay and the Pyrenees.

He knew roughly the size of Britain with a fair degree of accuracy. He knew the basic terrain. He knew its inhabitants were mostly peasant farmers, less civilised and less highly organised both in politics and war than the Gauls. He was confident that with a total of five legions at his command he would be able to conquer and subdue the inhabitants whom he understood were divided into many disparate tribes who spent much of the year at war with each other.

There were two other factors to consider. Caesar was mindful of the Druids and of their power and influence over the common man. He also respected their teachings and their intelligence. And he knew that the Druids were men of great influence in both Gaul and Britain. In the same way that some warriors from Britain fought in Gaul, so he understood that Druids would cross quite freely from Gaul to Britain and back again as though there was little difference between the two countries.

And one other reason suggested is the fact that Rome wanted jurisdiction and control over the whole of Europe and that included the islands of Albion, the most western outpost.

In the autumn of 56BC, Caesar ordered his forces to

build 20 galleys which he planned to use for his light auxiliary forces to make the crossing to Britain. Traders from Britain and Gaul who constantly criss-crossed the channel throughout the year reported to British tribal chiefs that Caesar was building a small navy. They believed the only purpose of such a navy was to attempt an invasion of Britain.

In the summer of 55BC, Caesar had been occupied in Germany putting down a major rebellion against his forces after the Germans had agreed peace terms. Caesar believed this was 'treacherous and insidious' behaviour and vowed to teach the Germans a lesson. Within 24 hours of the Germans' surprise attack and victory against a small Roman force, Caesar immediately gathered his Army and marched on the Germans' main camp where 400,000 soldiers were billeted. Many in the camp were drinking, feasting and celebrating their victory with their women and children and camp followers.

Bursting into the German encampment, Caesar's legionaries and cavalry showed no mercy towards the treacherous Germans. Within two hours, all defence had been overthrown amid terrible slaughter and the German soldiers abandoned their women and children, threw away their weapons and their standards and fled towards the River Rhine in a desperate bid to escape. But there was no escape. Hundreds more were put to the sword while others desperately tried to escape, throwing themselves into the river where they perished, overcome by wounds, terror, weariness and the force of the current.

Throughout the summer of 55BC, Caesar was engaged

in bringing together his navy and learning all he could about the British tribes. Traders arriving in Gaul from Britain were immediately brought to the Roman general's camp and closely cross-questioned. He wanted to know the names of the tribes and the size of their forces, their method of fighting, their manners and their customs and, importantly, what harbours were available to accommodate a large flotilla.

Not satisfied with the answers he received, Caesar sent one of his lieutenants, Gaius Volusenus, in a single galley with instructions to make a reconnaissance, find a harbour, check the lie of the land and return in five days. As a result, at the beginning of August, Caesar ordered his cavalry and the Seventh and Tenth Legions, together with archers and slingers, to gather in and around Boulogne ready to embark on the 20 galleys and 80 transport ships that had been prepared for the invasion. There were a further 18 transport ships which were reserved for the horses.

In the hope that he might avoid any war against the British tribes, he sent envoys across the channel to urge as many tribes as possible to submit to the renowned Roman general. Some tribes suggested they would submit and offered a number of slaves, but only a few responded enthusiastically to his offer of peace in exchange for submission. Caesar feared that he might have a battle on his hands but he still had no real idea of how strong, brave and efficient the tribal warriors would be.

It was a fine night in late August when Caesar set sail. The moon was past the first quarter and the wind fair, but light and fitful. The crossing was uneventful but shortly after dawn the sailing ships became almost becalmed and Caesar arrived off the coast of Dover shortly after 9.00am. He was annoyed to be confronted with the towering white cliffs which he knew would make a successful landing very difficult against an efficient fighting force. After calling his officers to assemble on his ship, he made known his plans. The ships weighed anchor and sailed north-east until they found a favourable shore on which to land. In the event, Caesar's Army first made land between Walmer Castle and Deal Castle. He ran the ships aground on the gently sloping beach. The great Caesar had arrived.

From the moment the Roman armada of more than 100 ships appeared on the horizon, their every move had been closely followed by the four tribal leaders who had decided to repel Caesar and his Army before they could make a successful landing on British soil. As Caesar ordered his ships to sail north, they had been followed by the British cavalry, charioteers, archers and slingers.

But there was a problem. It was all but impossible to beach the large transport ships successfully because of their size and weight. So the ships were unable to make the shore and were grounded still in deep water, making it virtually impossible for the soldiers to unload equipment. With their heavy, cumbersome armour, shields and swords, the legionaries knew that if they came under sustained attack, they would face real difficulty in making their way to dry land.

Minutes after the legionaries began to disembark in the deep water, the British tribes, led by four tribal leaders, struck. And they were a fearsome force.

Thousands emerged over the brow of a hill and ran screaming and yelling towards the beach where the Roman forces were taken unawares as they struggled through the water to make the shore. It was a ferocious sight for the legionaries. The tribesmen, their shoulder-length hair flowing in the wind, their all but naked bodies painted in the traditional blue dye called woad, and wielding spears, swords and slings, raced down the beach towards the floundering legionaries. Hundreds of the attacking force were on horseback and many others were in small, two-wheeled chariots, pulled by a pair of horses. The chariots carried two men, the driver and a well-armed soldier often carrying an axe or a ball and chain as well as his sword and shield.

The horsemen and the soldiers came roaring down to the water's edge, hurled their spears and sling-shot at the Roman soldiers unnerving the usually well-disciplined Roman ranks who were taken aback by the intensity of the savage-looking barbarians. The legionaries began falling back into deeper water under such an onslaught and Caesar feared many would drown unless he acted quickly.

He ordered his light galleys, which had much less draught, to row hard along the shoreline away from the battle and then pull into the beach so that his auxiliaries could use spear and slings from the decks and his archers could keep up a withering attack on the enemy's flanks.

But it was the bravery of the standard-bearer of the Tenth Legion who was given the credit for saving the day. Seeing the enemy retreat out of range of the Roman archers, he stood on the deck of his transport ship and shouted above the noise, 'Leap down, men, unless you want to abandon the eagle to the enemy. I, at all events, shall have done my duty to my country and my general.'

He then threw himself into the shoulder-high water and advanced towards the enemy, bearing aloft the eagle on his standard. His bravery encouraged others to follow suit rather than face the ignominy of losing their legion's standard and, within minutes, hundreds more followed, leaping into the waters.

But that act of courage resulted in a titanic struggle in the shallows with the brave Britons battling to repel the Roman legionaries before they could reach dry land. Time and again the tribal leaders sent bands of warriors to surround a group of Romans who had just leapt into the sea, causing confusion. The legionaries, of course, found it virtually impossible to fight in the deep water, an experience they had never previously encountered.

Seeing the problem, Caesar ordered his small boats, called scouts, to row as fast as possible to whichever group of soldiers were being surrounded by the enemy and to drive them off. Slowly, Caesar's forces pushed back the British warriors until they had succeeded in reaching dry land. As soon as sufficient numbers of legionaries could re-group, they charged the enemy and put them to flight. But that was all. Caesar had no cavalry available to pursue the warriors and put them to the sword, which was Caesar's customary method of achieving a ruthless victory and, at the same time, humiliating and destroying the enemy.

Caesar, whose reputation was feared by the British tribal leaders, had won his first victory on British soil.

Within 24 hours, the defeated tribes had decided there was little point in trying to throw the Roman legions back into the sea and they dismissed their soldiers, sending each man back to his farm or village. They also sent envoys to Caesar to sue for peace, promising to give hostages and to obey his commands. They agreed to hand over 200 men, many of whom were transported directly to Rome and sold as slaves, never to return to their homeland, never to see their families again.

But luck was not on Caesar's side. His total lack of experience of the tidal differences around the coast of Britain cost him dear. To be fair, Caesar's seafaring experiences had all taken place in the calmer waters of the Mediterranean where there had been far less tidal flow. The night after the British tribes had promised to submit to the Roman legions, the moon was full and the tide almost at its spring high. It seemed that not one of Caesar's advisers, generals or sea captains had realised that there was a connection between the two events. As a gale struck the coast, the large rollers raced up the shingle and filled the hulls of Caesar's beached galleys; some of the transport ships dragged their anchors and were dashed on shore as the helpless Romans looked on aghast.

In the morning, Caesar surveyed the damage. The beach was littered with wreckage, the shattered hulls and the smashed remains of his navy. The rest had been rendered useless by the loss of their rigging, anchors and other fittings. There were no facilities for repairs, no spare tackle and no more ships which Caesar could call upon to rescue his Army. Intending only to stay briefly in Britain in order to make contact with the tribal chiefs and survey the land, Caesar had brought no supplies to maintain his men through the winter.

This state of affairs was also witnessed by the tribal chiefs who determined to starve out the Roman legions, cut off their men from corn and other supplies and continually harass them. The British chiefs were confident that if they could overpower Caesar's Army or prevent their return to mainland Europe, no invader would dare to attempt to conquer Britain for many, many years.

To feed his troops, Caesar ordered soldiers from the Seventh Legion to go into the surrounding fields to reap the corn and bring it back to camp along with timber. The timber would be used not only for repairing the ships but also to provide wood for fires. The British warriors watched the Roman soldiers at work day after day until there was only one small patch of corn to be cut. That night, the warriors stealthily took up positions in the dense forest nearby and, when the warriors had laid down their arms and had begun cutting the corn, the tribal warriors, their bodies again dyed in woad, emerged from the forest and fell upon the hapless legionaries.

Attracted by clouds of dust, the Roman look-out reported to Caesar that the legion might have come under attack. Fearing the worst, Caesar called his troops together and took off for the corn fields. He found his troops hard pressed and under severe pressure from the British cavalry and war-chariots, as well as suffering from attacks by archers and slingers.

This was the first time that Caesar had seen such war-chariots in action and was so impressed by this method of warfare which he had never before heard about that he later wrote about them in his commentaries.

'Chariots are used in action in the following way,' he wrote. 'First of all, the charioteers drive all over the field of battle, the warriors hurling missiles; and generally they throw the enemy's ranks into confusion by the mere terror inspired by their horses and the clatter of the wheels. As soon as they have penetrated between the troops of cavalry, the warriors jump off the chariots and fight on foot. The drivers meanwhile gradually withdraw from the action, and range their cars in such a position that, if the warriors are hard pressed by the enemy's numbers, they may easily get back on them. Thus they exhibit in action the mobility of cavalry combined with the steadiness of infantry; and they become so efficient from constant practice and training that they will drive their horses at full gallop, keeping them well in hand, down a steep incline, check and turn them in an instant, run along the centre pole, stand on the yoke, and step backwards again to the cars with the greatest nimbleness.'

But Caesar had noted a flaw in their capability. The war-chariots were brilliant against scattered parties of infantry engaged in foraging or ravaging, but were not so dangerous when confronting a legion in tight battle formation. The chief tactical problem presented to him by the British charioteers was the difficulty of pursuit. Without a cavalry of his own, charioteers could always escape his legionaries when their attack failed, leaving them to fight another day.

Caesar's intervention saved the day, but he knew there was no chance of achieving a victory with his troops outnumbered by such a determined force. He succeeded in rescuing the great majority of his legionaries but the attack had left a number dead on the battlefield and many others wounded.

There followed five days of unrelenting rain and Caesar spent that time repairing his ships to make them seaworthy and encouraging his troops. But the heavy rain also prevented the tribes from following up their partial victory. They realised their chariots and their cavalry would not be at their most efficient in such rainy conditions. In the meantime, the four chiefs sent emissaries to other tribes further afield, explaining the situation and urging them to come and join battle with the Romans as they sensed victory. The tribal leaders responded hoping to drive the Romans from their camp and into the sea.

The British tribal chiefs did not care if they defeated the Roman legions on the sea shore or forced them to return to their ships and sail back to the European mainland. They believed that either course of action would bring independence to Britain for many years to come.

By the seventh day, the rain had gone and hot sun had dried the land. Shortly after dawn, a large number of British warriors arrived outside the Roman camp with cavalry, chariots, archers and slingers. Caesar drew up his disciplined legions outside the camp directly facing the taunting, yelling, shouting warriors who were waving spears and gesticulating with bows, axes and sticks. Battle commenced but the Roman legions, knowing that defeat would mean almost certain death, stood their ground as wave after wave of warriors attacked, only to be beaten off. The British cavalry and war-chariots could not be used in this situation and, as a result, the legionaries slowly gained ground. After the tribesmen had been repulsed a number of times, the Roman legions counter-attacked and the tribesmen turned and fled before them. The Roman infantry pursued them as far as their speed and endurance would permit, killing a good many of them. As dusk fell, the legionaries returned to their camp, burning all the buildings they came across.

That night, the tribal chiefs once again sent envoys to Caesar to sue for peace. He ordered them to surrender twice as many hostages and immediately despatch them across to the continent. When some of the British hostages had set sail, Caesar immediately struck camp and taking advantage of fine weather and calm seas, he decided to risk the sea crossing in his battered and partially repaired ships. He feared that waiting for the ships to be properly repaired might take so long the crossing would become even more difficult as winter set in. Neither was he certain that the tribal chiefs wouldn't attempt a further attack. In fact, all the ships reached the continental ports safely but, Caesar noted, the British never sent the promised number of hostages.

On his return to Gaul, Caesar called his shipwrights to a meeting and explained that he wanted them to build a fleet of several hundred ships, but they would have to be differently constructed to the ones they customarily built for use in the Mediterranean Sea. Caesar ordered that the new vessels would be a little shallower than usual transports and also wider-bottomed to carry as many stores and provisions as possible. He explained that the new ships should be able to be loaded more rapidly and should be capable of being hauled up on shore unlike the transports he had sailed to Britain. All these vessels he ordered had to be constructed both for rowing and sailing. Amazingly, 600 of the new type of ship were constructed through the winter, an epic achievement.

Once again, the British tribal leaders had learned from traders that Caesar had ordered a great armada of ships should be built in Brittany throughout the winter months and they learned in the summer of 54BC that Caesar was gathering a great Army with which he intended to conquer the British Isles. Caesar's fleet of 28 warships and 540 transports set sail from Boulogne in July 54BC and arrived on the shore near Sandwich in the late morning. The British tribes had been waiting, prepared to attack Caesar's legionaries before they had time to disembark. But, with their newly designed ships, the Romans were able to sail their vessels virtually on to the beaches so the troops could disembark in shallow water. On seeing the vast armada safely beach on the shore, the tribes fell back to plan another course of action.

Caesar decided to surprise the British tribes hoping to engage and destroy them in one great strike. He left the coast some time after midnight and made for Canterbury, where prisoners taken that evening believed the tribes were massing for an attack. He found the British forces defending an ancient fort called Bigbury on the brow of the hill two miles west of Canterbury, overlooking the river Stour. Caesar's cavalry roamed the area, comfortably dealing with any cavalry or charioteers they encountered. Meanwhile, the Seventh Legion attacked the fort. Though the ramparts rose 20 feet above them, the legionaries locked the shields of the front rank of soldiers while their comrades piled a mound of earth. Within hours, they were in a position to charge the fort. The defenders were no match for the seasoned legionaries and within hours the tribesmen had fled the fort.

For once, the Roman troops did not follow in hot pursuit for Caesar judged that after the sea crossing, the night march and a hand-to-hand battle, his troops were in no condition to march and fight in a strange, inhospitable country. He pitched camp.

It was fortunate for Caesar that he had done so. He was woken at dawn with the dramatic news that once again the sea and the wind had caused mayhem for his fleet. He rushed immediately to the Small Downs off Sandwich where his ships had been riding at anchor while some had been drawn up on the beach. Caesar was aghast at the devastation that confronted him. Most of the ships at sea had dragged their anchors, and many had fallen foul of each other and had been thrown in their scores on to the beach to be hammered by the full force of the rollers. Some of the ships which had been deliberately beached had been smashed by the other ships and battered by the rollers. Forty of his ships were a total loss and those that could be saved needed substantial repair work. He set his skilled men to work repairing the vessels and sent a galley back to Gaul ordering his senior officer to build another 40 vessels.

But he feared that another storm might wreck the rest of his fleet. So he ordered every ship to be hauled out of the water and beached above the high water mark and then entrenched against possible enemy attack. It was a long, hard and arduous job for his troops and it took nearly two weeks. Understandably, the devastation of Caesar's fleet was greeted with delight and, more importantly, as a good omen by the tribal leaders. They believed that for Caesar's fleet to be struck twice in 12 months by gales and heavy seas was a sign from the gods that he should never have attempted to invade and conquer Britain. To many, the wrecking of his fleet proved that Caesar was not invincible and gave hope that, as the year before, Caesar would be forced to withdraw once again and leave the islands to the British tribes. As before, Caesar's ill luck encouraged the Britons to renew their resistance against him for now they were convinced that the gods were on their side.

Despite these omens, there were others who realised that defeating Caesar and his legions would be a monumental task for the reputation of his legions was known throughout southern Britain. Caesar's record of innumerable military victories throughout Gaul and Germany had been spread far and wide and the British kings, tribal leaders and war lords had little doubt that Caesar was determined to conquer the islands and bring them under the control and authority of the Empire.

It was at this point that the Kentish tribal kings sent emissaries to other tribes further north and west telling them of the Roman invasion and urging them to send warriors to defend the country. More importantly, they also appealed to Cassivellaunus, king of the chief tribe among the recent Belgic settlers from northern Europe, the Catuvellauni. This tribe, the spear-point of the Belgic invasion, had pushed across the Thames above London and was consolidating its position throughout what is now Hertfordshire.

The Catuvellauni capital and the stronghold of Cassivellaunus was a fortress of 100 acres, protected by ramparts and a ditch 40ft in depth. This had been constructed on the hill beside Wheathampstead, a little north of Verulam. After some persuasion, Cassivellaunus agreed to take command of all the British forces in return for which he would contribute his entire Army, then considered to be the most powerful in the land, to the defence of Britain.

Within days of Caesar's bid to advance from the coast towards Verulam, he had met stiff resistance from cavalry and war charioteers. And every time Caesar's legions engaged the British forces, they would escape to the woods before turning against their pursuers and inflicting heavy losses. And when the Romans were making preparations to camp for the night, the British struck again.

Caesar was worried. He realised that the British were well led and their tactics highly successful. He reached the conclusion that his heavily armed infantry, though safe enough in battle formation, could never put up more than a passive defence against audacious and swiftly moving barbarians. Caesar had never fought against such a nimble Army before. He noted that 'the British barbarians', to use his words, had no regular formation but fought in isolated and mobile groups, each of which could be reinforced whenever necessary by fresh men. On occasions, the mobile groups would dissolve in a feigned retreat to lead over-eager pursuers on to their destruction. The nimble charioteers would retreat at speed, disembark and when the Roman cavalry arrived on the scene, the British would attack the bellies of the horses with their spears and swords, splitting open their stomachs. This caused the cavalrymen to fall from their mounts and they, in turn, were ruthlessly put to the sword.

Caesar retired that night to mull over a new form of warfare which would overcome the highly successful British tactics which were inflicting severe losses on his troops and damaging morale. A few days later, Caesar sent out nearly half his infantry of 2,000 men into the surrounding countryside to forage for wood, keeping back another 1,700 troops and all his cavalry. The over-confident Britons fell into the trap and attacked the foraging troops with reckless abandon. Caesar then released his cavalry, backed by the remaining legionaries, and they swept the British warriors and their charioteers from the battlefield. Caesar ordered his troops to continue chasing the enemy, never giving the charioteers enough time to stop, turn, dismount and fight. This single defeat sapped the confidence of many of the British forces who decided they would never defeat the Roman Army and returned to their tribes. Though Caesar was involved in other battles and skirmishes during his second invasion, that battle was the last full-scale general action against a massed British Army.

But Caesar was determined to follow Cassivellaunus to

his kingdom, annihilate his Army in battle and plunder, ravage and destroy his capital. Caesar believed that by destroying the Army of the great Belgic king, he would put the fear of God into all the other tribes whom, he believed, would then sue for peace. But first Caesar had to cross the great river — the Thames.

Cassivellaunus had kept a watch on Caesar's legions and cavalry as they tracked westwards and he heard from prisoners of the great general's plans to destroy his Army and his capital. He was determined to prevent Caesar's Army from crossing and therefore gaining a foothold north of the Thames — his tribal territory. Cassivellaunus drew up his entire force at the spot — believed to be at modern-day Brentford — where forces generally crossed. He fenced the opposite bank with sharp stakes and fixed similar stakes below the water line. It was all to no avail. The Roman cavalry and infantry, with the soldiers up to their necks in the deep water, forded the river with such speed and brio that the British tribes took fright, turned and fled. With Cassivellaunus's forces defeated, Caesar believed he had the British tribes at his mercy.

The Trinovantes tribe, enemies of the Catuvellauni for a generation, did immediately send envoys to Caesar and sued for peace, offering 40 hostages and grain for his Army. Sensibly, Caesar agreed to protect the Trinovantes from the Catuvellauni and promised to take no further action against the tribe if they kept the peace. Caesar's diplomatic initiative spread quickly and, within a matter of days, five more tribes surrendered.

From the Trinovantes, Caesar learned the exact

location of the Catuvellaunian capital at Wheathampstead and took off at speed. He seemed to surprise the defenders who were not present in great numbers and, within two hours, had overcome the British warriors, putting every man they found to the sword. Caesar took hundreds of prisoners as well as all the cattle and pigs in the immediate vicinity. These he would take back to Gaul, selling off the captured soldiers as slaves to pay for the heavy cost of building his fleet, and keeping the livestock to feed his Army.

But the daring Cassivellaunus was not yet finished. He appealed to four Kentish tribes to attack Caesar's fleet still drawn up on the beaches and put it to the torch. He believed that it would be possible to contain Caesar and his Army through the winter, cut his forces off from wheat, corn and livestock, and then force him to sue for peace. Or so he hoped. But this plan too went quickly awry when the defending Roman soldiers comfortably repelled the rather weak British attack. Cassivellaunus sued for peace, offered hundreds of hostages, and a grateful Caesar accepted the terms. Word had reached him that some German tribes had become restless and had renewed hostilities against Roman forces. Caesar packed all his booty into the transports, including hundreds of slaves, cattle and pigs, and returned with all his forces safely to Gaul.

The British warriors watched from the cliffs of Dover as the last Roman ships set sail for Gaul, happy that the great Caesar had decided to return to the continent and leave them in peace once more. But now they knew that the very best British soldiers, and their most able general,

Cassivellaunus, had been soundly defeated. They worried that the great Caesar would return the following year with perhaps more legions and wreak havoc once again.

But, of course, he did not.

The British people were left in relative peace for nearly 100 years due to civil wars and political problems facing Caesar's successors as Emperors of the Roman Empire. It was almost inevitable that one day the Roman legions would return to Britain, and almost certainly with the intention of conquering the islands and bringing them under the power and influence of Rome.

* * *

For Rome and its great influential writers, there were fundamental beliefs and certain traditions that Romans held about their nation and of Rome's general attitude to the world.

The illustrious Roman poet, Virgil, who lived from 70–19BC, and who took 11 years to write the epic Trojan story of *Aeneas*, the legendary founder of the Roman nation, wrote:

> *'Forget not, Roman, that it is your special genius*
> *to rule the peoples; to impose the ways of peace,*
> *to spare the defeated, and to crush those proud men*
> *who will not submit.'*

In another poem, Virgil makes the supreme Roman god Jupiter declare, 'I set upon the Roman bounds neither of space nor of time: I have bestowed upon them empire without limit.'

And the contemporary Roman historian Livy (59BC–AD17) who was no friend of Caesar's, wrote the definitive history of Rome comprising an extraordinary 142 books. He wrote, 'Go and announce to the Romans … that the gods desire my city of Rome shall be the capital of all the countries of the world. To that end they shall cultivate the arts of war and transmit their knowledge to their descendants so that no human power shall be able to resist the military might of Rome.'

Claudius, who was Emperor of Rome from AD41–54, decided in early AD43 that the moment had arrived to conquer Britain once and for all. Britain was known to be rich in raw materials such as metals, wheat, cattle and, just as importantly, slaves. There was good reason to believe that, as a Province of Rome, it would well pay its way, able to sustain financially the legions necessary to keep the island docile. Claudius, considered by many in Rome to have been something of a buffoon, also wanted to win the praise and acclaim of the Roman people so, by invading Britain, he was emulating the great dictator and Roman hero, Julius Caesar.

Claudius entrusted the third invasion of Britain to Aulus Plautius, a general who had spent most of his career in Germany and Gaul. He was given four legions and a number of auxiliaries, a total of 40,000 men. At this time, legions had a nominal strength of 5,000 men and were divided into ten cohorts, each of 480 men, except the first which probably comprised 800. Each ordinary cohort consisted of six centuries of 80 men. The bulk of the legion was infantry and there were a few cavalrymen who acted as scouts and messengers. In each cohort a few legionaries were specialists — engineers, architects, masons, clerks, medical staff, cobblers, metal workers and other trades. Nearly all these specialist soldiers were highly trained, long-service professionals whose skills were as important to the Roman administration in peace as in war. The soldiers who invaded Britain in AD43 wore a newly designed helmet made partly of iron and designed with a better guard for the neck. The earlier corselet strengthened with metal had given way to more flexible body armour made of strips of metal. Under the armour the soldier wore a sleeved tunic. The only protection below the waist was a group of metal-bound thongs which was worn like a sporran. On his feet he wore studded boots akin to heavy sandals.

His shield, generally rectangular and curved to fit the body, was mostly made of wood, but fitted with a metal boss which could be used to throw an assailant off-balance by being thrust in his face. As offensive weapons, the legionary carried a pair of javelins, each equipped with a soft metal shaft below the head which was designed to bend when the missile stuck in an enemy shield. It could thus not be thrown back, and being difficult to pull out, rendered the shield useless. As his personal weapon, the soldier carried a short stabbing sword.

Legionary fighting tactics were based on close-quarter fighting with tightly packed, disciplined ranks where the short sword was more effective and easier to handle than the longer swords used by the British warriors. In siege warfare and, occasionally, in open battles, the Roman infantryman was supported by an assortment of missile-throwing machines, large and small catapults, some on towers which could be wheeled about the battlefield.

Besides the legionaries, there were also those officially described as 'auxiliaries'. Originally, they were non-Roman troops, often ill-disciplined, unreliable and, more often than not, likely to desert. However, the taking of vast territories throughout Europe and the Middle East provided a steady supply of soldiers who had fought against the Empire and were now willing to fight on behalf of Rome. These non-Roman soldiers were eventually organised into regular units, usually lead by Roman officers. It was under the Emperor Claudius that the reward for an honourable career as an auxiliary was to be granted Roman citizenship.

The 40,000 soldiers and a large contingent of cavalry who had been gathered at Boulogne at first refused to obey the order of Plautius to embark. They had heard many tales of ancient Britain, the islands at the edge of the world, which they had been led to believe was inhabited by wild men and wild animals. They had also heard of the many calamities that befell the seamen and the ships which dared to sail in the cold, harsh, gale-swept waters. The troops felt they were being sent beyond the known world to a mysterious land of terror and mystery. For two months, the troops continued their mutiny, refusing to embark and, in desperation in the face of such ill-discipline, Plautius had to send a messenger to Rome to obtain an edict from the

Emperor Claudius ordering the troops to obey their commander and sail to Britain.

Finally, the edict arrived, and the troops agreed to end their mutiny, for there could be no denying the order of the Emperor. The legions embarked at Boulogne as Caesar had done 90 years before. Unlike Caesar, however, Plautius decided to split his armada into three and land at three different sites in an effort to confuse the defenders. To the surprise of Plautius, however, this feint proved unnecessary for there were no British warriors to 'welcome' them and the armada finally reached the large, land-locked natural harbour of Richborough, hidden behind the Isle of Thanet.

The British tribes had heard that a large Roman fleet was being prepared at Boulogne but, for reasons unknown, convinced themselves that no invasion was imminent. As a result, the Roman legions landed without any resistance whatsoever and spent the first few weeks of their campaign in Britain marching and counter-marching across Kent searching for an enemy which they never found.

At the time of the Claudian invasion, the sons of Cunobelinus, Caratacus and Togodomnus, had succeeded their father only three months before. The kingdom had been divided betwen the two sons so both assumed responsibilities as king of their respective areas. Between them they ruled Cassivellaunus in Hertfordshire but also most of Kent and Essex where the local tribes had been suppressed during their father's reign. One of the reasons behind the decision to invade Britain in AD43 was the fact that following the death of the powerful Cunobelinus

(Shakespeare's prototype for Cymbeline) earlier that year, news had reached Rome that family and tribal quarrels, and internecine strife, were rife in south-east Britain.

Another contemporary Roman historian, Publius Tacitus (AD55–120) would write of the reasons for the successful Claudian invasion of Britain:

> 'Once the Britons were obedient to kings; now they are torn apart by the warring parties of different leaders. There is, of course, from our point of view, nothing more useful than if, when we are facing more than one strong enemy, they do not act in concert. It is very rare that two or more British tribes will come together to repel a common danger. They fight separately and separately are defeated.'

And that simple logic was the undoing of the British defenders. When news of the fresh invasion reached Caratacus and his brother Togodumnus, both men mustered their own forces and marched off to tackle the invaders. Caratacus reached Kent first and took up a defensive position on Caesar's old battlefield at the crossing of the River Stour. His defensive position was the best possible, yet the Roman forces easily overran the British warriors, crushing them in a matter of hours and then relentlessly driving them back as hard and fast as was possible. Caratacus only narrowly escaped with his life and he fled back along Watling Street towards his capital at Wheathampstead.

Worse would follow. As the Roman forces followed Caratacus and his ravaged Army, they came across

Togodumnus with his smaller force. Within two hours, they had swept through the defenders putting many to the sword. But the British weren't finished yet.

Those first two engagements were mere skirmishes and the large Roman force had not yet broken the spirit of the British warriors who still confronted their enemies from a distance, yelling obscenities and profanities which the Roman legions would never have understood. The British soldiers were an awesome-looking lot, waving their long swords in the air above their heads and taunting the enemy to attack. They marched up and down some distance from the legionaries with their near-naked bodies covered in woad and their shoulder-length hair flying in the wind, seemingly eager for the next engagement.

Caratacus and Togodumnus joined their forces together and messengers visited tribes in Kent and Essex urging their leaders to provide as many levies as possible in a bid to throw back the Roman Army. The British tribes responded and within a couple of weeks a large Army mustered once again on the Medway and encamped on wooded hills out of sight of the Roman forces. When they heard the Romans were advancing to challenge them, they crossed the Thames at Rochester where a bridge had been constructed. They burned the bridge behind them and made plans for a major battle against the Romans at a location of their own choosing.

But the Roman cavalry swam the Thames and charged the British charioteers who were caught unawares. Meanwhile, the Second Legion found a ford upstream and crossed to the northern bank, striking at the right flank of the British forces. But the attacks were beaten off by the courageous British forces and the generalship of Caratacus who out-manoeuvred the Roman high command. That day's battle was undoubtedly a victory for the British forces and Caratacus and his men wondered if such a defeat would persuade the Romans to retreat. In those times, it was customary that, after such a ferocious day's hand-to-hand battle, both sides would withdraw to rest, lick their wounds and plan the next battle. But not on this occasion.

The following day, the Roman forces returned to the offensive, surprising the British warriors who were regrouping for the next engagement. After initial preliminaries of screaming and yelling, the opposing forces clashed repeatedly, both sides charging, then falling back before charging at each other once again. Fierce hand-to-hand fighting involving thousands of men took place over a five-hour period before the Roman legions gained the summit of a ridge overlooking the battlefield. With the larger Roman force holding the high ground, the exhausted, disillusioned, though undefeated, British warriors fell back and retreated across the plain towards Colchester with the Roman legions in pursuit. That single battle — the Battle of Medway — would become the decisive engagement of the entire invasion.

The British warriors spent the next weeks and months watching the Roman infantry and cavalry from a distance as the Army made its way across Kent and Sussex in the south before crossing the Thames in substantial numbers and taking Essex, Hertfordshire and those parts of Britain north of the Thames to the Wash. There was virtually no opposition but the tribes in all those areas, numbering between 20 and 30 principal ones, were forced to submit, offer hostages and agree to provide the Roman Army with the provisions it demanded.

Throughout the Roman campaign, the British noted the discipline of the Roman forces as they steadily occupied more and more territory. And they watched the legions prepare and strike camp each and every day. Each Roman soldier carried two stakes which were used for the palisade inside a ditch which was dug at every overnight stop, before settling down to eat and sleep. Within this ditch, the tents were drawn up in formation according to a fixed pattern which never altered. As the Roman Army settled into regular garrisons along the route, these patterns were adapted to the standard Roman fort whose classic playing-card shape evolved in the course of the first century AD. When the Romans first invaded, the fort still had tents inside the defences, then it was furnished with wooden buildings and finally stone.

Even when encamped in garrisons, the soldiers were often ordered to practise laying out a fort, digging ditches, erecting tents and constructing defences. They were also ordered to assist the civil authorities in building projects, particularly in later decades when the Roman-built whole towns, bridges, siege-works and their remarkable roads. And the speed at which a legion could work was quite outstanding. On one notable occasion, four legions — approximately 20,000 men — constructed a substantial road nearly five miles long in three days!

The life of the British warrior was, of course, totally

different. There was no standing army and very little discipline. The great majority of the tribal armies that faced the Roman forces were simply drawn from the men who worked on the farms, producing food for their families. When faced with an enemy, the local warrior chief, leader or king would simply send runners far and wide to call together all able-bodied men to defend their families and their farms. When planning an attack, the tribal leader would gather together sufficient men for the battle plan and set off. The reward for those fortunate to return would be more land or some of the animals which had been captured during the attack. Some were rewarded with hostages, both male and female, who, in reality, were nothing more than slaves.

There was little or no basic training, only the haphazard learning by experience when engaged in tackling other tribal warriors in small, fragmented skirmishes. Unlike the Roman Army there was no drill, no basic discipline and no permanent structure of command. This meant that the Britons could not and did not carry out any manoeuvres in battle. Roman legions, on the other hand, could execute pre-arranged and well-rehearsed movements at the command of a trumpet, could be sent to other parts of the battlefield or could operate either as a single mass unit or resourceful individuals.

And the arms the British warrior carried were very basic. His weapon was the traditional, long Celtic sword, designed for combat in open battle where the warrior would have sufficient room to swing it about violently. He had no body armour whatsoever. Sometimes, warriors went into battle with only a small piece of hide around their middles, at other times with long, loose woollen trousers. Above the waist they were, more often than not, naked.

The more fortunate warriors, from land-owning and trading families, were expected to lead the farmers into battle with the king, the tribal chief or the local leader in command. Some of these men wore helmets and carried shields, some of which had been elaborately decorated. These leaders usually rode their horses into battle or used the famous chariots which singled out the British fighting force from any other encountered by the Roman Army anywhere else in the known world. These upper-class warriors must have practised on horseback, as well as trained in chariot driving and fighting, because the Roman generals, including Caesar, were struck by the expertise, courage and mobility of the charioteers which caused confusion in the ranks of the opposing armies.

And yet, despite such lack of discipline and virtually no drill or practice, the British warriors on occasions out-fought and out-manoeuvred the renowned Roman legions, though not for any length of time. It was accepted that the British warriors fought with tenacity and great courage, refusing to back off until overwhelmed by superior numbers. The feared Roman legions were not used to such courageous, stubborn resistance, for their enemies often turned and fled at the mere sight of the ranks of Roman infantry marching in disciplined order towards them.

The final act in the invasion of Britain was performed

by the Emperor Claudius himself. He had ordered Plautius to take the areas south of the Thames and then call a halt to the advance and await his arrival. Plautius obeyed and the Roman forces took up defensive positions south of the Thames, leaving the British forces to take whatever action they wished. Claudius arrived in Britain with his élite praetorian guard and, remarkably, a corps of elephants!

Slowly but surely, Claudius and his elephants made their way from the coast across Kent to the Thames and then to Colchester. He met little resistance. His triumphal arrival at Colchester, at the head of his praetorian guard, disciplined legions and corps of elephants was watched in awe and amazement by a few hundred British people, none of whom had ever seen an elephant never mind a Roman Emperor. Claudius received the submission of a number of tribes and laid down the terms for a peaceful settlement.

Claudius proclaimed that the kingdom was to be a Roman province with Colchester as its capital and Plautius as its first governor. The town of Colchester was a great disappointment to Claudius and his retinue who had only recently left the splendour of Rome. At that time, Colchester was little more than a large village with a few dozen wooden houses around which were the little wooden round-houses the great majority of the British nation were still using. There were no buildings of note, no public buildings and only a few small, single-storey forts constructed of rock and stone. As a consequence, Claudius proclaimed that the barbaric town would be burned down and a Roman-style city would be built on a hill south-east of the town. This would become the official residence of the Governor and the seat of the Roman government; and in the centre of the city, surrounded by the porticoes of a forum, a vast and massive temple would be built where Claudius would be worshipped for ever as a god!

Having accepted submissions from many other tribes, whose kingdoms ranged from the Sussex coast to the Wash, including the powerful Iceni tribe, Claudius decided to return to Rome and enjoy his reward — a magnificent, triumphal celebration which the Romans usually gave their victorious emperors returning from conquests far afield.

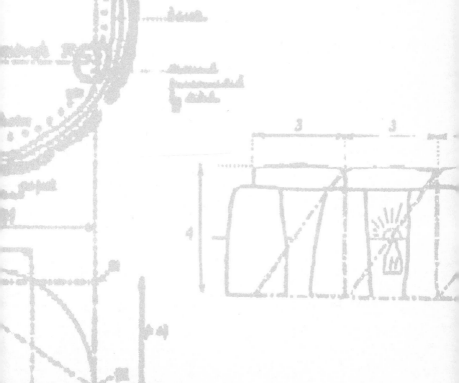

6.

REBELLION

One of the proudest episodes of Britain's history, taught to every schoolchild, was the audacious rebellion fought against the might of the Roman Army by the young Boadicea, queen of the Iceni tribe which inhabited an area of eastern Britain. But before Boadicea led her dramatic rebellion against the hated Romans, there were other tribal leaders who raised armies in a bid to expel the Roman legions from Britain.

Many of the tribes of south and east Britain had been shocked into inaction for the three years following the successful invasion of Britain in AD43. After gaining a foothold in the south-east of Britain, the all-powerful Roman legions had brushed aside the British tribes which had tried and failed to hurl them back into the sea and the tribes and their chiefs had retired back to their provinces to lick their wounds.

During those years, the Romans had built camps and garrisons in strategic positions in the east, the south and the midlands. They had subdued most of the tribes that had crossed their path, defeating some in quick actions and reaching amicable arrangements with others who had been prepared to settle on peaceful terms rather than take up arms against the all-powerful invaders. The legions had adopted the same policies that had won them such success throughout their relentless push westwards and northwards across Europe. They had built up their all-important supply lines, constructed well-protected defensive garrisons and continued to push further into mainland Britain, comfortably dealing with any tribes who tried to stand in their way. Slowly, the Roman legions took command of ever-increasing areas and many tribal leaders came to realise that there was little point in continuing a war of attrition against such a well-equipped and disciplined army.

But that was not true of all the tribes the Romans encountered.

In AD47, Aulus Plautius, a first-class soldier and general, and the first consul appointed to govern Britain, was recalled to Rome and replaced by another general, Publius Ostorius Scapula. Those tribes that had retreated towards the north in a bid to escape the Roman Army decided to use the change of consul as the best time to test the new commander and launched a series of raids across the conquerors. Mainly, the tribes used the classic hit-and-run tactics of guerrilla warfare and inflicted some serious casualties on the Roman legions.

But Scapula was no faint-hearted soldier but a man of action with a reputation for ferocity whenever it became necessary, and especially in defence of his beloved legionaries. As the tribal fighters struck at various garrisons, Scapula decided to strike back. He marched at speed at the head of a number of lightly armed cohorts — a division of the Roman Army — and ruthlessly stamped out all opposition. But in his attempt to end any possibility of further guerrilla war, Scapula would go too far.

Aulus Plautius had given permission for some of the tribes, including the Iceni, to keep their weapons so that they could defend themselves against any warring marauders who made their way across the North Sea to plunder and pillage the towns and villages in eastern Britain. He had also permitted those tribes to keep and farm their lands. Many other tribes who had taken up arms against the Roman invaders had not only been stripped of all their weapons but had also had their lands confiscated and officially became the private property of the Emperor. It was this heavy-handed method of dealing with the vanquished tribes that embittered them so much. Their entreaties to the Romans had fallen on deaf ears and, as a result, the tribes had resorted to taking up arms in a bid to reclaim their lands. It had, however, been a somewhat futile effort. Scapula decided that the Iceni had broken their word and decided to disarm not only the Iceni but also every tribe east of the River Severn. He reckoned that such action would remove any threat to his legions, who would never again face any serious opposition from aggressive British tribes.

Scapula also wanted to make the southern and eastern part of Britain a safe and peaceful part of the Empire in which Roman generals believed there was no need whatsoever for any tribes to carry arms or engage in any warring activity. Peace would be preserved and guaranteed by the presence of Roman legions. But that wasn't how the Iceni saw the forced surrender of their weapons of war.

The Iceni had been one of the most powerful tribes to accede voluntarily to the Roman side shortly after the invasion of AD43, and they bitterly resented Scapula's arbitrary decision to disarm them of every weapon they possessed. They had reached an agreement with Plautius and had kept their side of the bargain, handing over the agreed number of recruits for the Roman Army as well as paying their alloted tribute. Scapula had arbitrarily torn up the agreement and insisted that the Iceni hand over all their weapons.

The Roman legions were ordered to tour the entire tribal area, visiting the hamlets and villages and forcibly taking away every weapon they found. There were skirmishes and minor battles and each act of defiance was met ruthlessly by the Roman forces, massacring whole villages that dared to confront the legionaries. The action of Scapula was met by outrage and this quickly turned to hatred of the conquering Roman forces.

The Iceni joined forces with another aggrieved tribe, the Trinovantes, as well as some lesser tribes, and the tribal leaders decided that the time had come to rise up against the overbearing Roman forces and stake their claim to the sovereignty of the tribal area they had been promised. Battle was joined on a small natural island in the peat fens near March in Cambridgeshire. The tribal warriors decided that their only chance of success was to build strong fortifications and defend themselves against the expected Roman onslaught. They planned to launch counter-attacks with their charioteers. The tribes put up a stiff resistance but the disciplined Roman forces, backed by lightly armed auxiliaries brought from the south of the country, were too much for them and they broke through the tribal strongholds inflicting heavy casualties. The tribes fled the field of battle defeated and badly mauled, but they did manage to take most of their weapons. The Roman forces did not follow up their victory, fearing the Iceni and the Trinovantes would have more forces ready for action.

But the Roman victory spurred on the Roman general Ostorius who decided that the time was ripe to take harsh action against other tribes whom the Roman administrators believed might take action against them. His first campaign took the Roman legions to north Wales, a part of the country inhabited by the Decangi tribe where Roman soldiers and auxiliaries had never before ventured. He undertook no pitched battles but waited for the Decangi warrior to harass his column of troops. Then, Ostorius would issue orders for an immediate counter-attack, ruthlessly putting to the sword anyone they came across as they chased and harried the tribal warriors across country. As punishment, Ostorius sent his troops to loot Decangi towns and villages with orders to take away as much booty as they could carry. The Decangi were left in a parlous state, their young men cut down in battle and most of their treasures taken away. It had been a bitter lesson.

Encouraged by the gallant efforts of the Iceni and the Trinovantes, other tribes began to show their mettle, challenging the Roman forces whenever possible, mainly relying on the tactics of guerrilla warfare. Years before, the British fighting men had learned that there was no chance of defeating well-organised Roman legions or auxiliaries in open battle. Some tribes still trusted their age-old method of fighting from their chariots, darting at speed at columns of soldiers away from the main force and then ferociously cutting them to pieces before leaping back on their one-horse chariots and disappearing into the forest. The Roman forces knew from bitter experience that there was danger in following these charioteers into the forests because they knew they would lie in wait and spring a trap.

One of the most belligerent tribes which had taunted the Romans since their arrival in Britain were the Brigantes whose tribal lands covered a vast area between the midlands and the Scottish borders. Their Queen, a strong woman by the name of Cartimandua, had of her own volition made peace with Plautius despite strong opposition from her own advisers and generals. Bands of Brigantes warriors took the matter into their own hands and began raiding and plundering lesser tribes who had become totally submissive to the Roman soldiery. The wayward Brigantes would plunder their towns and hamlets and take away their women, their livestock and their slaves.

These smaller tribes turned to the Romans for

protection and Ostorius moved north with a powerful force to teach the Brigantes a lesson and try to persuade them to stop attacking lesser tribes otherwise they would face annihilation at the hands of his legionaries. After routing a Brigantes army that openly challenged him, Ostorius warned Queen Cartimandua that she had to be responsible for keeping her army in check or face the consequences. As a direct result, a few tribal leaders rebelled against Cartimandua and she informed Ostorius that civil war was brewing. He marched north once more, confronted the renegade warriors and swiftly defeated them, summarily executing some leaders and capturing many warriors whom he despatched to Rome as slaves. He also demanded a handsome tribute be paid to the Imperial coffers.

One of the Romans' most prominent and courageous opponents who had earned a reputation as a leader and a warrior was Caratacus, a strong, pugnacious young man. His father, Cunobelinus, was a member of the house of Tasciovanus and thought to be one of his illegitimate sons. The long struggle for supremacy among the various British tribes had finally been won by the Catuvellauni and, as a result, coins bearing the head of Cunobelinus, and then his son Caratacus, were struck.

By the year AD47, Caratacus had become the general in command of those tribes which still opposed Rome and he set up his headquarters in the territory of the Ordovices in Wales, where he hoped to be out of reach of the Roman legions. Following the Roman invasion four years earlier, when so many tribes had been routed, Caratacus had first retreated to Gloucestershire and had constructed the famous earth works known as The Bulwarks on Minchinhampton Common, one of the largest strongholds ever constructed against the invaders. Here, he gathered as many tribes as possible under his banner hoping to win their support for a concerted war on the Roman legions. Caratacus orchestrated a classic guerrilla war against the Roman legions, only taking part in surprise raids and causing fear and confusion among the invading force. But, as the Romans steadily moved further westwards, Caratacus and his Army had been forced to flee to the relative safety of mid-Wales.

Here, Caratacus also took over as leader of the Silures, a fierce, proud tribe noted for their belligerence, their wild demeanour and their refusal to bow before the Roman legions. From here, Caratacus continued his campaign of guerrilla war. He continually attacked and destroyed the small garrisons and police-posts that the Romans had set up along the River Severn. And each garrison that was over-run by Caratacus and his forces was wiped out and destroyed. As a result of all this activity, Caratacus became a national hero, worshipped by his followers as the champion of their liberty and their heaven-sent leader against the hated Romans.

Ostorius decided that the only way to counter the constant guerilla tactics was to garrison as many Roman legions and auxiliaries as possible near the Welsh border, forces that would be quite capable of defending themselves and delivering a severe beating in any major battle. As planned, the Roman forces pressed on relentlessly, dealing ruthlessly with any forces that opposed them. But the

Roman generals found great difficulty in successfully putting down the Silures. No matter what action the Roman legions took against the tribe, nothing seemed to have any lasting effect. Ostorius tried both harsh and lenient treatment, but to no effect.

But the relentless move westward finally had an effect on Caratacus and his warriors, forcing them to retreat towards mid-Wales. Caratacus feared that Ostorius was building up his forces for a major confrontation with his rebel Army and decided that he would need to establish first-class defences in a battleground of his own choice if there was to be any chance of defeating the professional, well-disciplined Roman legions. However, Caratacus believed the headstrong, courageous Silurian warriors were exactly the kind of forces required to tackle the Roman legions.

As word of his intention to form a large army spread among the tribes, more came to join his forces in Wales, far away from the areas under the control of the legionaries. Over a period of three months, Caratacus, the Silures and the Ordovices were joined by other tribes and agreed to fight under the command of Caratacus. All who dreaded the idea of a Roman peace came to his side.

The Roman pacification that the tribes feared was to become notorious throughout rebellious Britain: 'they make a desolation and call it peace'.

Within a few weeks, the gathering of tribes came to the notice of the hated Ostorius and he set off with a powerful army of legionaries and auxiliaries to put down what he believed was the most serious threat to have confronted the Roman forces in Britain. He had been warned that if the Roman legions fell before the combined might of the British tribes, retribution would be swift and ruthless with the massacre of thousands of his soldiers. He realised that there was no love lost between most tribes and his own legions. He also feared such a defeat might well put an abrupt and highly embarrassing end to the Roman occupation. He did not want to be known in Rome as the general who lost the island of Britain, for such ignominy would bring a dramatic halt to any future prospects.

Ostorius would have known the fate that would befall him if he was recalled to Rome to face the Senate and explain the reasons why he had failed to hold Britain. His career would have been in ruins, his public humiliation would have been deeply embarrassing to his entire family and he would have probably faced exile to some tiny, unimportant, nondescript Roman outpost where he would have been left to rot.

Caratacus was forewarned that Ostorius was moving west to confront and destroy the Army Caratacus had formed. So he decided to act swiftly. The site of the all-important battle was chosen by Caratacus who had been handed command of all the rebel tribes that had gathered together to join battle with the Roman legions. Caratacus had marched his troops from mid-Wales to a battle ground he had discovered months before on the River Severn.

He marshalled his troops on a range of craggy hills above the river looking eastwards, its summit ringed by a stone wall fort overlooking the river. He quickly commanded his troops to build another rampart to fortify their position. To the rear of the British forces was difficult country, almost impassable to a large body of men trying to move at speed and thus making the prospect of being surrounded by Roman legions almost an impossibility. Caratacus was thus protected from the front by the River Severn and from the rear by difficult terrain and he would have the commanding position, looking down upon the Roman legionaries.

Caratacus had learned that a legion in line of battle was almost invincible to the British warriors with their disciplined, shifting formations. He calculated, however, that no troops, no matter how well drilled, could keep shoulder to shoulder while advancing over steep and broken ground. Caratacus believed his wild skirmishers stood every chance of repulsing any Roman charge before it reached the walls of the fort where his last stand would be made.

But Ostorius had arrived at the scene of battle well prepared, bringing with him a great force of troops, out-numbering Caratacus's warriors by two to one. Caratacus's tactics were to stay put in their defensive positions which appeared almost impregnable both to Caratacus and Ostorius. He anticipated the Roman attack, which he believed he could easily repulse, would become exhausted and dispirited after failing repeatedly. When the Romans finally fell back exhausted, Caratacus planned to swarm down the hill and cut them to pieces.

The battle began with taunts and yells and challenges from the warriors overlooking the Roman legions below. Ostorius was reported to have been dismayed by the situation and called a conference of war asking the opinion of his centurions. He even asked whether they should consider withdrawing to a more suitable battle site and wait for the tribal warriors to come down from their advantageous position. His officers would hear nothing of such a plan, arguing their legionaries were quite capable of fording the river and taking out the warriors who appeared out-numbered, ill-equipped and ill-disciplined compared to the Roman legions and auxiliaries.

The British tribes barely moved as the Roman legions began crossing the river and, within a space of a couple of hours, a large Roman force was on the other bank, looking up the gentle gradient to the screaming warriors who were hurling spears, rocks and stones down upon them. The Romans then began a flanking movement, marching both left and right, away from the tribal warriors and then climbing the gradient and turning towards Caratacus's Army, waiting for the attack to begin. A major part of the Roman Army stayed below on the river bank so that Caratacus and his forces were under attack on three sides. Every advantage which Caratacus had carefully planned had been thrown away by the decision to stand and defend rather than attack the Romans.

Battle was joined with the tribal armies facing legionaries both to the left and right and below them. The Roman auxiliaries' first attack took them across the river and nearly to the top of the slope where they came to a standstill as the British warriors hurled spears, rocks and missiles on the heads of the Romans. Their only protection were their shields which they placed over their heads.

Here the discipline and steadfastness of the Roman soldiery paid dividends. While some auxiliaries held aloft their shields others tore at the fort's stone work and tore down the walls in three different places. As the Romans breached the walls the Britons tried desperately to hold their ground but were forced to retreat to the very summit of the hill. Here, surrounded and hopelessly out-numbered, the remnants of the defenders retreated while others tried to make good their escape, running back through the almost impassable country, their only avenue of escape.

The defeat became a near rout as the legions closed in on the frightened, indisciplined tribal warriors. Many were put to the sword as they tried to flee through the undergrowth. Indeed, those camp followers, many of them women, who had marched with their menfolk to witness the annihilation of the Roman forces, were also caught up in the rout and Caratacus's wife and daughter were captured. They were taken away in chains to an unknown fate. His brother was forced to surrender and Caratacus himself fled north to the protection of the Brigantes, the one British tribe which he believed might yet be capable of tackling and defeating the Roman armies.

Caratacus appealed to Queen Cartimandua of the Brigantes to join the British tribes opposed to Rome, telling her that without the large Brigantes Army there was no chance of victory. Cartimandua, however, had decided long before to throw in her lot with the Roman invaders and was conscious of the fact that the Roman governor had come to her assistance when confronted by open rebellion by her own tribes. So she promptly arrested Caratacus, threw him in chains and personally handed him over to Ostorius as a pledge of her loyalty. He immediately despatched Caratacus under armed guard to Rome.

This capture of Caratacus was considered a great triumph by the Roman Senate and he was ordered to make an appearance before the assembled senators and later before the Emperor Claudius. Caratacus was seen to be a man of stature and answered questions thrown at him with dignity and honesty. The populace took to this soldier, believing him to be a king among men and, as a result, his life was spared and he ended his days in honourable captivity in Rome.

With Caratacus safely in Rome, Ostorius and his advisers believed the threat to the Roman conquerors had all but disappeared. The pledge of loyalty from the Brigantes tribe and the destruction of the armies under Caratacus, including the wild warriors of the Silures, led the Roman legions into a false sense of security. It would not last for long. Ostorius then made a simple error of judgement for which he and many legionaries would pay dearly. He began treating the conquered Silures and the other, smaller tribes as conquered, vanquished people of little regard, to be treated as slaves. Ostorius ordered the construction of forts and garrisons throughout mid-Wales and the Roman soldiers treated the Silures with disdain.

But the Silures were only waiting for the right time to strike, to avenge their leader Caratacus and the insults handed out to them by their Roman conquerors. When the Roman soldiery had been moved into the forts in various parts of Wales, the Silures took their opportunity and the whole tribe rose up. A number of recently built forts were attacked, the soldiers killed and the forts dismantled. And when the small Roman detachments of soldiers were sent to relieve their hard-pressed comrades, the Silures sprang traps, putting to the sword all those who couldn't escape the net.

The Silures had found the spirit to avenge their earlier defeat and were determined to inflict as much damage as possible on the Roman forces. On one occasion, they overwhelmed a large foraging party and cut to pieces the cavalry sent to rescue them; they then routed auxiliary infantry sent to rescue the cavalry and only fled when Ostorius himself appeared at the head of a large detachment of legionaries. But even then, the Silures managed to escape into the dusk with very little loss of life. Ostorius was rattled. Such attacks continued across central Wales and, by swift, well-timed attacks, the resilient tribe inflicted heavy losses on the Romans.

The Silures had learned their lesson in the defeat of Caratacus. Never again would they stand and do battle with the Romans, for that way only led to defeat and humiliation. Instead, they would carry out Caratacus's original and highly successful campaign of guerrilla warfare. The Silures became ever more confident, sometimes carrying off plunder and prisoners, sometimes carrying out wholesale slaughter of Roman soldiers they caught in a trap. Their spirit was only heightened by learning that the Roman governor Scapula had sworn to exterminate the entire tribe.

Other tribes began to take note of the extraordinary

successes of the Silures and they decided to join their cause. It was at this point that Ostorius, worn out by constant wars and battles and unable to quell the upstart tribes, took to his bed and, unexpectedly, died. Before his successor, Aulus Didius Gallus, could arrive, the military situation deteriorated rapidly. Astonishingly, the Silures had defeated the famous Second Legion in an open battle and the Silures were destroying forts and garrisons far and wide. A born leader, Didius, already in his fifties, knew he quickly had to restore the initiative or there was a real danger of defeat. He realised that if Britain was lost to the Roman Empire — defeated on the field of battle — he would be recalled to Rome in ignominy.

Prasutagus, king of the Iceni, had submitted to Claudius in AD43, the year of the conquest and, as a result had been allowed to keep his throne as a 'client' king. When Prasutagus died he left a widow, Boadicea, and two daughters, and it was understood that Boadicea would succeed her husband. But the notorious Nero, who had been proclaimed Emperor in AD54, had other ideas. Nero proclaimed that the royal line of Iceni had become extinct and all its property was to be confiscated. Nero went further, proclaiming that the property of all the Icenian noblemen should be confiscated and he sent a procurator to sack the Icenian royal palace.

The Norfolk palace was attacked by a large band of armed Romans and everything that could be taken — jewellery, gold, silver, ornaments, carpets and furniture — was removed. When Queen Boadicea protested she was taken outside, stripped naked and publicly flogged. Her two daughters were repeatedly raped by members of the armed band of Romans. Noblemen and relatives of the late king were seized, put in chains and taken to Rome where they were sold as slaves. Some ended up literally fighting for their lives as, to entertain Emperor Nero, they were thrown to the wild animals in the amphitheatre in Rome.

The entire Iceni tribe was held to ransom. Debts incurred in the process of 'Romanising' Icenian society — involving large purchases from the traders who followed in the wake of the legions — were called in by panicky financiers forcing most of the noblemen, landowners and wealthy farmers into debt. And in the midst of this ruin and outrage, the officers of the Roman government appeared demanding more young recruits for the Army and more tribute money for Nero. No argument was permitted. Every order was carried out in the name of the Emperor. The young men were either taken away to join the Roman Army or sent with their sisters to Rome to be sold as slaves. The entire region was incensed at what was happening, furious at the breach of faith and terrified at the prospect of endless oppression at the hands of Rome. Burning to avenge the insults to their royal family and furious at the treatment of their sons and daughters, the Iceni implored Boadicea to take up arms against the Roman tyrants.

The famous Roman historian, Dio Cassius, wrote a striking description of Boadicea:

> 'In stature, Boadicea was very tall and grim in appearance, with a piercing gaze and a harsh voice. She had

a mass of very fair hair which she grew down to her hips,
and wore a great gold torque [a necklace of twisted
metal] *and a multicoloured tunic folded round her, over*
which was a thick cloak fastened with a brooch. This was
how she always dressed.'

She approached the Trinovantes tribe which had
settled around Colchester for she knew they were smarting
at the treatment meted out to them ever since the invasion.
The Trinovantes had a special hatred of the older,
discharged Roman legionaries who had retired to
Colchester. These veterans drove the native inhabitants
from their homes and farms and treated them as slaves and
captives. They were happy to throw in their lot with the
Iceni.

The Roman veterans in Colchester caught wind of
rumours of a possible uprising and called for armed
support. Two hundred lightly armed men were dispatched
to guard Colchester as a precaution, but the veterans were
still sceptical that anything serious was afoot. They did not
even bother to evacuate non-combatants, such as the
women and children, a normal practice in such
circumstances.

Within days of the 200 armed defenders arriving at
Colchester, the Iceni and Trinovantes, led by the enraged
and vengeful Boadicea, struck. Boadicea had received
reliable intelligence of conditions inside the city from
native residents who had lived there for some years. The
intelligence was so accurate and detailed that Boadicea's
tribal leaders knew where the defenders would take up

positions when under attack. One significant fundamental fact was that, unlike most major towns and cities, Colchester had no defensive walls though it did boast a range of well-equipped public buildings — a council chamber, theatre and a huge temple dedicated to the Imperial Cult of the Roman Empire. This temple, a symbol of the servitude to which all Britons had been reduced, was hated and villified by Britons opposed to the Roman Empire. Rebels within Colchester not only resented the ordinary taxes levied upon them but, especially, the demands made upon them for the upkeep and service of this temple, the symbol of Rome's dominance in their midst.

As dawn broke one spring morning, the citizens of Colchester were awoken by a cacophany of screaming warriors who had completely surrounded the town and were now running wildly into the town centre. The few Romans who had weapons fled to the temple whose massive stone base was the only thing that could resist the impending sword and flame. The rest of the town was systematically torched, with every house, every building, every market stall burned. Within hours, the entire town was a mass of flames and when it eventually died down, nothing was left except the blackened hulk of the temple and its few score defenders. Within 48 hours, that, too, had succumbed, the defenders being mercilessly put to the sword.

At Lincoln, the Ninth Legion, commanded by a gallant officer, Quintus Petillius Cerialis, set out on a forced march in a desperate effort to save Colchester. Quintus

Petillius, with his 2,000 men, never arrived at Colchester. He was met on the outskirts of the town by Boadicea's Army of 7,000 tribal warriors. Swamped by the sheer weight of numbers, the legionaries went down fighting. Once again, no Roman soldier was spared though Petillius and a few cavalry men managed to escape.

News of the dramatic sacking and burning of Colchester spread throughout the Roman hierarchy in Britain, so much so that some generals and senior administrators, fearing for their lives, believed the Roman Army was about to be soundly defeated and thrown out of Britain. On hearing the dramatic news of the great Iceni victory and the wild rumours that were sweeping the country, these men collected their families and immediately travelled to the nearest sea ports where they boarded any ship they could find and crossed to Gaul.

At the time Boadicea struck at Colchester, the Governor, Gaius Suetonius Paulinus, was encamped 240 miles away in Anglesey with both the Fourteenth and the Twentieth Legions. But his main depot and supply base were in London, where he feared Boadicea and her warriors might strike next. He decided to take his cavalry and gallop flat out for London, leaving the infantry to follow at all speed. He sent three horsemen to Gloucester to summon the Second Legion which was encamped there. Wherever he rested to change horses, Paulinus heard news of towns and villages being sacked and torched by the rampaging Iceni Army which was attracting hundreds more warriors to their cause along the route.

In AD60, London was a large, peaceful town full of

traders, Roman administrators and merchants. It was also Rome's principal port in the British Isles where all goods and supplies for the Roman legions were brought from Gaul and was, as a consequence, utterly incapable of defending itself. The supply depot was, however, entrenched and pallisaded and guarded by a handful of veteran troops.

Within 48 hours of arriving in London, Paulinus heard that Boadicea's Army was heading south and London was their target. He heard that the Second Legion had decided to stay in Gloucester rather than risk a heavy defeat. Paulinus knew there was no hope, whatsoever, of saving the town and he decided to abandon it and its inhabitants to their fate. Extraordinary scenes took place as traders and merchants with their women and children begged and pleaded with Paulinus and his 200 cavalry men to take them to safety. There were at least 1,000 people screaming and wailing in the streets, begging Paulinus and the cavalry not to abandon them to the enemy. But Paulinus knew that his duty lay in returning to his faithful legions and, if possible, leading them against the rebels in a bid to ensure that Britain remained part of the Empire. The odds against Paulinus achieving a victory against such a wild, vast army, hell-bent on killing and retribution, were slim. With his cavalry, Paulinus took off up the famous Watling Street in search of his legions and made contact with them in a forest 50 miles north of Verulam (St Albans).

Two days after Paulinus had fled London, Boadicea arrived with her tribal armies. The massacre of every man, woman and child who had any connection with Rome or the Roman occupation of Britain, including merchants and traders, their families and their children, was carried out systematically by the warriors. There was no resistance whatsoever and no prisoners were taken. The vast majority of the 50,000 people massacred were killed by the sword but some were hanged from gallows while others were crucified. Many died in the inferno that raged for days when the town was put to the torch after the killing had been completed. (There was a site in Spitalfields where the bones of people were found in the 1920s which appear to have been buried by the cartload. Archaeological evidence appears to prove that these bones were the remains of the Roman settlers who perished during Boadicea's massacre.)

But Boadicea had not yet completed what she believed to be her duty. Leaving some troops in London the great bulk of her Army turned north and marched on Verulam which was then Rome's main administrative centre in Britain. Many people tried to flee the town but without success and Boadicea's warriors put the town to the torch after killing and massacring every single person who had any connection whatseover with Rome. Both in London and Verulam, neither the women nor the children were spared. The massacre was total. In Colchester, London and St Albans, more than 70,000 men, women and children were killed either by the sword, the gallows, crucifixion or the ensuing fire. All three towns were left burning ruins with hardly a building still standing.

Then Boadicea took off in pursuit of Paulinus whom she knew had quit London to rally his legions for one final stand against her victorious Army. It now totalled some

20,000 warriors, but numbers had more than trebled because many of her men had brought along their women and children who followed the Army in horse-drawn carts and wagons.

Paulinus had only 10,000 men under his command and he knew that, if he did not win this forthcoming battle, then Rome's 17 years in Britain would be at an end. His men also knew from the reports of the massacres of the other three towns that if they did not defeat this rag-tag army of wild warriors, they, too, would be cut down until no one was left standing.

Paulinus, however, did have sufficient time to plan his defence and placed his legions on a field of battle where his flank and rear were protected by dense woods, ensuring that the enemy would have to attack his front line. He also placed his cavalry out of view behind the woods where they could strike at the enemy flanks. Boadicea and her over-confident warriors drew up their wagons opposite the Roman front line, intending to trap the legionaries. As the Britons were making preparations for the battle ahead — gesticulating, screaming and shouting in an attempt to terrify the legionaries — Paulinus ordered his men to charge. With swords drawn, the legionaries ran straight at the hordes of ill-disciplined warriors while the cavalry struck at both flanks. Taken by surprise, Boadicea's gallant warriors were thrown on the defensive, and they fell back in confusion on to their own wagons drawn up behind them.

The result was carnage. The warriors were trapped between their wagons, loaded with women and children, and the disciplined Roman force of some 10,000 battle-hardened legionaries. Men, women, children and even the horses were cut down amidst the most appalling screaming and mayhem. For four hours the legionaries, covered in the blood of their enemy, ploughed through the morass of dead bodies, killing anyone they found still breathing. It had been the most appalling slaughter. Boadicea took poison and died before the slaughter was complete. The great, spontaneous rebellion was at an end.

A terrible vengeance followed. For the next six months, Roman legionaries were sent into the lands of the Iceni and the Trinovantes, as well as other suspect tribes in eastern Britain, to ravage the towns and countryside and slaughter those suspected of supporting the great rebellion. No one was spared. The revenge continued for six terrifying months until it was brought to a halt on the orders of Nero.

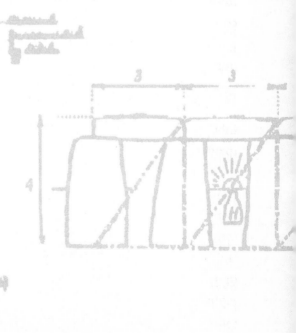

7.

LIFE IN THE NEW BRITAIN

One hundred years after Year Zero, much had changed for many inhabitants of Albion, particularly for those living in the south and east of the British Isles who had borne the brunt of the changes brought about by the successful invasion by Roman legions in AD43. The occupation of the island by the Roman legionnaires had taken place over a number of years as the Roman Army pushed north towards Scotland and the Irish Sea.

During the first 20 years of occupation, little changed throughout the land as the Roman forces were still fearful of attack from a number of recalcitrant tribes. Massive concentrations of the Roman forces still centred mainly around the major towns of the south-east.

As late as AD60, Roman forces would venture out from their fortified camps only warily in an attempt to pacify the local people and, if possible, start trade and gain the confidence of the unfriendly locals. Various forts and many blockhouses had been erected in the midlands and the west country, but the Roman soldiery were still not entirely confident of their safety.

The Roman consuls knew only too well that their first objective was to persuade and convince the native aristocracies that their interests lay with Rome rather than leading their tribes against such a powerful foe. This was, in effect, the beginning of the 'Romanisation' of Britain. But the Roman official classes, both military and civil, and the eventual creation of a unified substructure of urban society, were the mainsprings which came to influence the local economy.

But the idea that the Romans came to Britain and constructed towns, cities, superb buildings and a wonderfully efficient road system for the benefit of the local citizens of Albion was far from the truth. Indeed, the occupying Roman legions didn't, in fact, undertake any work for the local population, not even defence works. In the Roman world order, amenities for civilians were expected to come from the pockets of private citizens and not from the coffers of Rome.

The only buildings constructed by the Romans were for their own occupation; the public buildings they constructed were only for Roman administration; and the only forts and defences constructed were for the Roman armies. Even the bath houses, which were eventually erected near most Roman towns, were only for the use of the Roman Army and civilians and not the local people. The famous roads built by Roman soldiers, which were to last centuries, were only built to speed the movement of Roman troops.

Indeed, some of the practices carried out by successive Roman consuls in Britain caused much anger and resentment among the local aristocracy and tradespeople for, far from being advantageous to the locals, they were quite the opposite. One such disadvantage was that, in some areas, the local tribes had to buy back grain at inflated prices that they had already supplied as taxation in kind in order to fulfil their quotas. They were often ordered to deliver the grain to military encampments far away and usually where there were no roads. Most locals found a way round the problem by bribing the Roman officials, which was probably the whole idea in the first place.

But even 100 years after the Roman legions first arrived in Britain to settle the islands, there were still pockets of resistance much to the annoyance and frustration of the occupying forces. The Roman governor Julius Agricola, who ruled Britain from AD78–84, began his term of office by taking a large force of troops and marching through mid-Wales determined to smash the powerful Ordovices tribe which for decades had attacked and harassed the Roman legions.

In fact, Agricola all but annihilated the tribe in an appalling massacre in which legionnaires went from village to village killing every man, woman and child they could find. The few families who managed to survive had escaped to the mountains. But the settlements in that area of Wales did not recover for 200 years. By this dramatic use of terror, Agricola established himself with his troops, the province and any potential enemies.

Agricola then turned the other cheek, encouraging local aristocrats, the farmers and the rabble of young men who lived by offering their services on the battle ground to put their faith in Rome. He seduced and bribed them, offering them the pleasures of life, encouraging them to build temples and bath-houses, public squares, public buildings and modern houses in the towns the Roman administrators decided should be constructed. Agricola drafted in Roman architects, professional advisers and engineers to help design and construct these buildings, as well as instructing the local people eager to learn and follow the Roman way of life. By such subterfuge, Agricola eventually won great acclaim across Britain for the Roman lifestyle.

Agricola then set about encouraging greater education than the Druids themselves had practised, suggesting that all children of aristocratic and land-owning families should receive a full education. Within a decade, those who had shunned the Latin language sought fluency and eloquence in it. The leaders and elders of the various tribes learned Latin and became fluent speakers. Latin was the key to a more privileged life in Roman Britain, for it became the language of law and public administration in the same way, centuries later, that English became the *lingua franca* of India.

In time, most Britons became almost completely

Romanised; their children learnt to recite Virgil at school, potters wrote their scrawls in Latin, brickmakers used it as a matter of course. The greatest influence on the spread of practical Latin was the Army. Not only did a Roman soldier need to speak Latin, he also needed to be able to read it.

The more the Roman soldiers mixed and fraternised with the locals, the more Latin spread throughout the nation. As a result, it became the spoken language at many levels of society. It is accepted that education in Britain was better under the Roman Empire than at any time since its fall until the nineteenth century. There were schools in Britain in the second century AD.

As the great English historian Gibbon wrote, 'The language of Virgil and Cicero, though with some inevitable mixture of corruption, was so universally adopted in Britain that the faint traces of the Celtic idioms were preserved only in the mountains or among the peasants.' Celtic certainly survived, as is obvious from the existence of Welsh and Cornish today.

Those who lived in the fast-burgeoning towns even adopted Roman dress and the toga was frequently seen. Over the following decades, Britons became more Romanised — some would say more civilised — enjoying the bathing houses, the assembly rooms and smart dinner parties. Roman influence changed the very lifestyle of the upper echelons of British people, encouraging the land-owners to move to the towns, away from the countryside.

The stated Roman objective was to persuade Britons to move from their scattered dwellings, become educated in Roman ways and take part in public life, which in Roman terms was a city-based concept. Earlier Greeks had spoken of their cities being divine and of themselves as being 'in love with her'. The Mediterranean world has always been a world of town-dwellers. Politically and socially the civilisation of the Mediterranean depended on the life of the town and Rome exported this idea throughout its far-flung empire.

Julius Caesar grasped and stated once and for all the essential character of contemporary British life when he said that Britain was rich in people and cattle, and covered with farms, but that all they had for towns were tracts of woodland fenced against assault. These hut-clusters were in no sense the nuclei of British civilisation for they were not so much cities as slums. To convert Britain into a province of the Roman Empire was to civilise it in the most literal sense of the word — to furnish it with towns.

Roman governors took it as their duty to educate the British to that end, insisting that it was vital that Britons should take a stake in the town, build a house for example, even if they retained a dwelling in the countryside. No one suggested Britons should give up their country estates, since the possession of land was an essential ingredient of being a Roman gentleman, but they always considered the town or city to be the proper focus of life.

Because Romans so enjoyed the social life of great towns, they wanted to encourage Britons to enjoy the same lifestyle which was so very different to the village life which had dominated the country from the first settlements centuries before. Roman philosophers believed that man's bodily and animal existence might be satisfied by country life but his spiritual needs could only be satisfied by the town. The town was considered to be both the symptom and the symbol of all that was highest and most precious in human life, all that raises man above the beasts of the field.

The Romans would attain this end by encouraging and helping the native Britons to build towns and even entire cities. Tribal senates were encouraged to adopt Roman town-planning schemes with chessboard street plans and handsome buildings. Occasionally, money would be lent from the Roman coffers, advice proffered and technicians brought in to advise and teach.

All these towns and cities were, in effect, very small despite their imposing buildings. London became the grand showpiece but contained only 330 acres within its walls. Other cities built in the decades following the Roman invasion included Lincoln (200 acres), Gloucester (230 acres), Cirencester (240 acres), Wroxeter (170 acres) and Verulam (St Albans) (200 acres). Most of the towns only covered around 30 to 40 acres.

None of these towns or cities were bustling affairs filled with throngs of people, for much of the space inside the walls was open and most of the buildings had ample spaces between them, including the large wooden houses. Only a small proportion of the population moved into these towns, the vast majority remaining on the land outside. Save for the magistrates, the aristocrats and the landowners, most of the town's population was made up of slaves and maids and the carpenters and artisans who were in great demand. Most of these towns, save for London, had populations of between only 2,000–4,000 people. London only boasted a population of 15,000 by AD100.

And in each town there were a smattering of shops which would always include a baker's, a blacksmith's, a saddlery and leather works, a stone-mason's and an iron and bronze works. There were also shops selling pottery and earthenware, glassware and woodwork, ranging from tables to chairs to cabinets and chests.

The houses were mostly large, detached and spacious. The best had perhaps 20 rooms, seemingly all on one floor, and most were about 20 feet square. The walls were frescoed and under-floor heating was common. Here, a rich man would live with his extended family and large retinue of slaves. The house, usually very square and angular, would be surrounded by a small garden and a gate would open out on to the street. But the local houses had no bathrooms, though those built for the Roman hierarchy always boasted a generous bathroom.

Apparently, the local dignitaries would troop off to the public baths where they would meet their friends and exchange the talk of the day. They would then go through the ritual of the Roman bath — the undressing, the cold room, the warm room, the hot room and then back. This would be followed by a massage and a cold shower before dressing and returning home for dinner. Most of the water for the public baths and the private houses came from wells dug nearby.

During these early decades of Roman occupation, Britons were subjected to other influences from Rome as soldiers from across the Empire were sent to Britain on tours of duty. Also, Roman judges and magistrates, doctors and lawyers came from all parts of Europe, North Africa and the Middle East and stayed in Britain for months, and sometimes years, bringing their influences to bear on the local population.

Having subjugated the rebellious tribes and having set about constructing a first-rate, though basic, metalled road system, the Roman governors began building towns at places where the Roman Army had settled. Some of the town's major administrative buildings, which Romans would use, were constructed by Roman architects and engineers with the help of local craftsmen and labourers.

The streets inside the towns and cities were well paved and well drained and were provided with pavements for pedestrians. These fine buildings were usually town halls, basilicas, law courts and judgement houses adorned with decorative columns, floors of marble, courtyards paved with mosaics and walls decorated with colours. In such surroundings, British lawyers argued their cases before Roman civilian administrators. They learnt the meaning of Roman justice, and they learnt the details of Roman law.

A forum was usually built for trade and doubled as a public meeting place. At a handful of sites, an amphitheatre for sports was erected to entertain the soldiery and there was a record of the occasional theatre being built in some towns for drama and religious rituals. Some of these theatres were quite small open-air affairs, while others, like the one at Canterbury, could house most of the 7,000-strong population of the town.

The single most important change which had an impact on the entire population was the fact that vast tracts of the country were living at peace with one another. No one living in Britain had ever experienced such continuous peacetime. Raids, skirmishes, battles and incessant wars had been fought out across the country for as long as anyone could remember. That was the reality of everyday life and had been for centuries. There were, of course, occasional periods of peace which might last for a few months or a few years, but there had always been the pervasive fear that an enemy could and would strike at any time.

There was a perpetual fear that the settlement, the village or whatever would be visited by men from a hostile tribe or some foreign army bent on rape and pillage, plunder and most important of all, the taking away of all the young men and women to be sold into slavery. Those left behind would know that they were unlikely ever to see those captured and taken because the majority were dispatched to the nearest port and shipped to Gaul or Germany where they were sold as slaves. Some were taken as far as Rome to be sold in the highly priced markets there. Slavery had been a lucrative trade in Europe ever since the Roman Empire had stamped its mark across the western world and Britons had become highly valued.

Most Britons were some five or six inches taller than the average height of the people of Rome and other southern Europeans. Those young men and women who arrived on the continent appealed to the Roman citizens because of their Nordic looks, their pale skin and long, blond flowing hair. The vast majority of people in the

Roman Empire were from a Middle Eastern background, southern Europe or north Africa — small, often thick-set men and women, dark-skinned with dark hair. The Britons fetched good prices.

It was a truism that all roads led to Rome. The Roman Empire was the greatest and most successful Europe had ever known. Virgil, the poet, made the supreme Roman god Jupiter declare, 'I set upon the Romans bounds neither of space nor of time: I have bestowed upon them empire without limit.' He also wrote:

> *'Forget not, Roman, that it is your special genius,*
> *to rule the peoples; to impose the ways of peace,*
> *to spare the defeated, and to crush those proud men*
> *who will not submit.'*

The Romans believed they had moral right on their side. If you were a non-Roman people, you were considered either dependent or proud and recalcitrant. It is this doctrine that explains why Romans felt they could treat minor kingdoms in their power exactly as they wished. It was also the reason Roman generals believed it was entirely permissible to exterminate whole tribes who proved intractable. Romans never recognised that there were areas of the known world over which they had no legal or moral right to govern, if they could physically enforce subjugation.

By AD100, the Romans had set up their proven machinery of government in the British Isles. Each main tribal area, of which there were then approximately 16, had a council which met at the principal town of the region, called the *civitas capital*. Membership was restricted to the land-owners. More importantly, an efficient tax-collecting system was set up. It was never forgotten that one of the main reasons for conquering Britain was not only simply to extend the Empire but mainly to trade in animals, dogs, minerals and slaves.

The tax system was set up to ensure that the cost of the 100,000 soldiers, administrators and other 'government' officials brought over to Britain was not paid for by Rome but by the British population. The main source of revenue was the land-tax, based on a survey dividing land into private property, communal property and state property and classifying it according to productivity. In addition there was the hated poll tax levied on every adult in a conquered population as well as a levy of grain for the maintenance of the occupying Roman legions.

And then there were the Customs duties levied on all goods passing across imperial frontiers. But because the Roman Empire was a great and highly successful common market, most goods arriving or leaving Britain would stay within the European market and therefore no taxes would be levied. However, all other international trade was subject to Customs duty, though many escaped duty because the ships used ports and harbours which weren't under the constant watch of the Roman Customs officers.

Towns were governed and taxed by a quasi-senate, called *ordo*, whose members were ex-magistrates. The *ordo* was loosely based on the Roman Senate. It was a permanent executive body of men which dealt with the ordinary business of the town by decree. The magistrates were elected by the town's adult citizens but apart from this single privilege citizens had no voice in public affairs. The *ordo* could and did raise taxes within the town at their own discretion. The sensible *ordo* were always mindful not to squeeze the townspeople too hard or they would pay the consequences.

The various British tribes were encouraged to follow the Roman lead without question, building towns, including a capital city for each tribe, which would be governed by a tribal *ordo*. For a generation after the conquest of Britain, each town was more or less run as a complete microcosm of the Roman constitution. Eventually, all these townships settled down into a standard constitutional pattern of a municipality, but none of them enjoyed Roman or even Latin citizen's rights.

As the century following the Year Zero neared its end, the great majority of the British population lived in the lowlands of southern Britain in an area bounded by the east coast as far as the Wash, the southern coast as far as Cornwall and then from Bristol directly across the midlands to the Wash. It was these lowlands that fell under the greatest Roman influence, there being little Romanisation in all other areas of Britain. It has been accepted that at this time there were probably 500,000 people in the lowlands, including probably 100,000 legionnaires, camp followers and others attached to the Roman armies, and another 500,000 at most in all the other areas of Britain, totalling about one million.

For the first 50 years, the centre of the Roman

influence throughout Britain was the Roman camp. Outside the large Roman towns set up in cantons — the subdivision of the country into major areas — the majority of Britain as far north as the Pennines was under the authority of the Roman military. Surrounding the Roman camps and forts were makeshift hamlets in which, apart from the farming community, the civilian population lived. In many respects these people, including men, women and their children, traders and skilled workers, were little more than camp followers, earning a living from assisting and supplying the needs of the Roman soldiery.

These major Roman camps or barracks usually held about 5,000 or more legionnaires and all their equipment, horses and enough food to last a winter. In that way, the Roman soldiery could be safe in the knowledge that they could hold out against any enemy without the risk of losing troops who might be attacked if they ventured out of the fort in search of food during the long British winter.

There were lesser camps holding only a couple of cohorts of troops and cavalry, perhaps 1,500 men and 'blockhouses' which were, in effect, outposts manned by less than 100 men. Even in the last years of the first century — around AD80–90 — these outposts continued to be targeted by some of the British tribes still determined to try and rid Britain of the Roman invaders. Such small tribal efforts, however, were of little significance after the great rebellion led by Boadicea had been ruthlessly put down.

Within the ramparts of the large camps, everything was arranged by the military with little or no regard for others living inside or immediately outside the barracks. Generally square, though occasionally rectangular in shape, the Roman fort was surrounded by ditches and earthen ramparts lying outside the wall. The corners were rounded and the four sides contained one gateway each. The corners were strengthened by towers or artillery platforms. From north to south a wide road cut through the centre of the fort and in the main street was the general's headquarters. These very large forts and camps were nearly always commanded by a Roman general.

The forts and camps differed in size and construction. Some were well fortified, entirely surrounded by walls, some as high as three men. These large, well-fortified forts were sometimes $800m^2$ while others were much smaller. Outside these forts were earth mounds and ditches with spiked staves providing protection for the inhabitants. Other camps were fenced with little protection but these were usually in areas where there was little prospect of enemy attack.

The headquarters building in the large forts comprised an outer courtyard surrounded by pillars and opening on to the wide main street on one side and an inner courtyard on the other. The inner courtyard was divided into a number of rooms, some used as regimental offices, while the centre one contained the regimental colours and a statue of the Emperor. Below ground level the money chest was kept in a stone cellar.

On one side of the headquarters building was the granary or regimental store house and next to that the fort's workshop. Close to these buildings was the commandant's house where his wife and family lived along with his own personal slaves which often numbered five or six men and women. On the same side of the main street were the officers' quarters and the drill-ground and stables; on the opposite side were the men's quarters usually made of wood or stone and divided into small compartments, each occupied by four or six men who slept and ate their food together.

Immediately outside the walls, usually near one of the four gates, was the all-important bath house, built of stone and capable of holding forty men or so. The bath house was always considered an important part of any military establishment, not only as a place for the soldiers to cleanse themselves but also designed to keep their muscles fit and supple. It was also a sort of club where the soldiers could sit around, chat and play games of chance.

The Roman legionnaires lived in some luxury when they were not actually engaged in fighting the enemy. In Britain, the ordinary Roman soldier had become used to coming under sporadic attack. Some tribes refused to bow before the Roman yoke and continued to harass and strike the legionnaires whenever an opportunity arose. In some respects, of course, the Roman forts provided the aggressive British tribes with the perfect target.

The Roman generals realised they needed to care for their soldiery because of the constant threat to their lives. It was one reason why the soldiers' quarters were far better than 90 per cent of the living conditions of the British population. Those wealthy land-owners and families with large farms who employed many slaves lived in beautiful large villas on their estates, but they were very few and far between. Most people still lived in the same wooden round-houses that their parents and grandparents had used before them.

The Roman soldier wanted for nothing. Under watchful guards, soldiers would work daily in the fields surrounding their camps, sowing crops, reaping and harvesting, looking after their sheep, cows and pigs in the same way as most Britons. But the Roman soldiery was provided with many more farming implements than the peasantry. Most of their tools and equipment was made from iron while the British still relied on wooden implements which wore out quickly.

The soldiers were noted as good, hard workers and they certainly knew what they were doing. At the end of the working day the soldiers would return to the safety of their forts and enjoy good food cooked for them. They ate off tin plates and used knives. To many British families, the Roman soldiers lived a good life, never short of food or any supplies. And most drank wine or mead out of goblets and tankards.

The Roman generals lived like mini-emperors and in far greater luxury than anyone living in Britain around the Year Zero. They employed senior soldiers who worked as senior civil servants making sure their master's orders were carried out. The generals and senior officers also owned many slaves, both men and women, who worked in their homes and in the headquarters. These men brought their wives and families over from Europe, as well as young women who worked with the family as maids and nannies. They ate splendidly, enjoying five-course meals which might take them an hour or two to finish and, throughout, they would drink fine wines.

Quite frequently, the generals would invite local aristocratic families to impress them and seduce them into adopting the Roman way of life. Even the plates and goblets, specially imported from others parts of the Empire, were richly decorated. Some ate off gold dishes. Sometimes a whole spit-roasted piglet or lamb would be brought to the table for a special banquet, though not usually in large numbers. At night, the rooms were lit by clay candles. And the general's home, and especially the dining halls, were warmed by the Roman method of central heating, pumping hot water around pipes under the floor.

And it was not only the general and his family who wore fine clothes. The legionnaires enjoyed good, warm clothes, even when working in the fields. They would wear leather shoes when the great majority of people in Britain wore rough sandals, some made from tree bark or wood. The womenfolk and the slaves usually wore material wrapped around their feet in winter but during the summer months they would generally walk around barefoot. The legionnaires' clothes were well made and their togas kept them warm during winter.

Slaves were universal throughout the Roman Empire as they were throughout the ancient world. Slaves were considered an absolute essential for people of position and power and even most households above a certain station had their own male and female slaves to help around the house or the farm. Slave girls and women usually cared for the children, cooked the food and cleaned the house. Slave men were used for all manner of manual work and would receive food and shelter in return.

For the great majority of slaves, life was hard. They had virtually no rights, and were the sole possession and property of their masters who had absolute control over them — literally, the power of life and death. They were bought and sold on the whim of their masters and any money received for them would go to the master. The treatment of slaves was also the sole right of the master who could have a slave flogged or branded. It was not unusual for a slave girl to be whipped for providing a poor meal.

But under Roman law, slaves could earn their freedom. And some slaves did manage to attain relatively high status in the local society working as officials in the Roman administrative system. Many slaves were freed after ten or twenty years' service but never before the age of 30. These slaves were known as 'freedmen' and 'freedwomen' and they continued to have a legal relationship with their former owners after being freed.

It was also seen as an enviable privilege if a slave girl's owner took her to his bed, and many children were born from such relationships. Ownership of the offspring would automatically pass to the slave girl's master and would be brought up as part of the household, not necessarily with any special privileges. However, because the very life of all slaves was at the whim of their masters, it was not unknown for such offspring to become senior members of the household with all the privileges that entailed. Slaves who revealed a high degree of intelligence were sometimes passed to those civil servants who ran the Empire on behalf of the Roman Emperors and, on occasions, such 'freedmen' could and did become powerful senior servants.

Fascinated and intrigued, the local people would go to see the soldiers at their bath house where there was both hot and cold water. The soldiers would strip off their clothes and bathe together, with perhaps 20 men or more sharing the same small pool. None of the British peasantry or even the aristocracy had seen such bath houses in their lives before. They were large stone buildings with roofs, some being decorated inside with marble and floor tiles.

Around the edge of the bath were wooden and stone benches on which the soldiers lay in the heat of the steam from the hot water. At that time, British people washed in water tubs where the rain collected and in summer they would wash and bathe in ponds, streams and rivers. But no one bathed in warm water. The only hot water was to be found in the pots for cooking or the kettles for drinking.

Slowly, bathing became attractive to the British people from all walks of life and wealthy land-owners began erecting bath houses adjacent to their properties. Following the lead of the Roman soldiery, people of all backgrounds found the bath houses attractive places for relaxation and bathing. There were charges for wealthy townspeople but soldiers, children and slaves were allowed free entry.

At first, the bath houses quickly became the sanctuary of lovers. No one wore clothes in the bath house and in a short time the bath houses of Britain became notorious for all the pleasures of the flesh. Much frolicking, abandonment and licentiousness was recorded and the bath houses soon became the sex centres of the towns much to the surprise of the Romans who considered the public bath house a respectable place of rest, relaxation and sport. Indeed, sports — particularly ball games, wrestling and a form of boxing — were great attractions in the bath house.

People would eat the equivalent of today's fast food — usually shellfish, cockles and mussels — as they lay around enjoying the heat of the steam. They would watch the young men wrestling and fighting and the soldiers would watch the naked young women bathing. Many people enjoyed the massages offered for which the masseurs would receive a small payment. And the bath houses were noisy places; not only were those selling drinks and food calling out their prices, but many of the games being played were watched by enthusiastic vocal spectators. Card games and dice were also played and betting took place mostly among the legionnaires. And there were always numbers of naked children racing around shouting and calling to one another.

But the increasing sexual activity of the bath house became too much in some Roman towns and public meetings were called in an effort to put an end to the hedonistic behaviour. In some towns, a separate bath house was built for the girls and women. At other towns, the decision was taken that men and women should only use the bath house on alternate days. But some towns simply turned a blind eye to the cavortings of the local people who, in any case, were still very open about all sexual matters.

The lives of the average peasant family hadn't changed with the arrival of the Roman legions. Whole families still lived cheek by jowl in their little, one-room, wooden round-houses where open sexual activity took place in front of the children. And there was still the same open relationship between the sexes with the men having sex with whichever girl or woman they fancied within the confines of the hamlet. The men still shared their womenfolk amongst themselves and no one had much idea of the fatherhood of any particular child.

The children simply grew up as part of a family, treating the men and the women as their parents and protectors. And the sons continued to have sex with the young girls and elder women, including their mothers; and the daughters were obliged to have sex with any of the men, young or old, fathers or relatives. They had no say in the matter. It would be 100 years or more before such circumstances changed for the poverty-stricken villagers.

In the towns, the ever-present legionnaires brought a sense of peace and calm which had never before been experienced on such a large scale. They acted not only as protectors and a defensive force but also as a police force whose duty it was to keep the peace at all times. The legionnaires always appeared well-disciplined, smart and highly efficient.

Whenever they left the protection of their camps and ventured into the surrounding countryside, they seemed impressive, marching in lines, carrying their swords in scabbards and spears on their shoulders. Some also carried shields which many decorated, some in bright colours. Some soldiers wore metal breast-plates and nearly all wore metal helmets. Because the helmets were heavy, the legionnaires would generally carry them.

Some of those who lived and worked within the forts and camps at a variety of jobs, from scribes to carpenters, from saddlers to iron workers, also brought with them wives and children from their last posting. Some senior legionnaires were also permitted to bring wives with them. The legionnaires were from all over the Empire but, as time wore on, most of the replacement soldiers were ferried across to Britain from Germany.

It was some time after the first 100 years of occupation that Britons were permitted to join the Roman Army. The soldiery served varying amounts of time in Britain but the majority stayed for five years before being replaced. Some soldiers chose to settle in Britain but the majority returned to their homes or took up posts in another legion elsewhere in the Empire.

Many of the ordinary soldiers, however, would consort with the camp followers. Some women followed the troops wherever they were stationed, whether in Gaul, Germany or Britain, and many had children by the soldiers. There were a number of young teenage peasant girls who, understandably, were attracted to the well-off legionnaires and were happy to throw in their lot with them.

Some married the legionnaires while others simply lived with one or more accepting the consequences of becoming pregnant. There were also many female camp followers who were simply harlots, but these were not welcomed by the Roman officers who feared disease would strike down their men. After leaving the Army, some legionnaires remained in Britain, settled down with a British wife and never returned to their homeland.

And yet, during that first 100 years following the successful invasion, life continued much as before for the great majority of the British people. Even when the towns were at the height of their prosperity, by far the largest part of the population lived in the country, either in villages or isolated farm houses. It is accepted that during this period more than two-thirds of the population were actively engaged in scraping a living from the land and they lived the ordinary peasant life which had not changed much for hundreds of years.

The villages were still a small muddle of huts, not houses. They were still one-roomed wooden constructions and circular in shape, in which an extended family might live huddled together. The village might consist of half-a-dozen or 30 such huts, thrown up in clusters and nearly always situated near a stream or a pond. Their farmed pieces of land would invariably be close by and their animals corralled either in similar huts or in a compound protected from wolves by earthworks.

The wealthy owners of country villas cultivated large open fields, while the poverty-stricken villagers tilled small, enclosed parcels of land, suggesting that strict tenures were in operation. The livestock kept by the owners of country villas included horses, cattle, sheep, pigs and geese. A villa with these provisions meant that the family could keep itself in bread, meat, milk and cheese, wine or beer, wool for spinning and weaving, raw leather, timber for burning and joinery, tallow for candles — in short, everything required for self-sufficiency and a full life. On the other hand, it seems the poor villagers, who were, in effect, tenant farmers, only had the means to keep the odd pig which would have to last the family throughout the winter months.

But the great majority of the British population was made up of peasants who barely eked out a living. Their main objective in life was to grow wheat in their small fields and, if fortunate, the family would own a pig, a sheep or a cow which could graze on nearby common pasture land.

The clusters of huts forming the village would be surrounded by earthwork defences, not so much as protection against human enemies but against wolves. Their huts were either wattled or thatched. Some were built beehive fashion in stone but the design or construction hadn't changed in centuries and the Roman influence hardly touched their lifestyle.

But the arrival of the Roman legions, which put a halt to further invasions and inter-tribal warfare, brought an instant and remarkable leap in the population. Suddenly, the warfare which had ended in the deaths of so many young men and the tribal raids which captured the young men and women and took them away as slaves, came to a dramatic halt. Within a matter of a few years, the villagers found themselves unable to feed all their young.

The young women would usually produce one child every year and now the little round huts could not hold the new, large extended families and the sparse village food supply could not feed all the extra mouths. As a result, infanticide became a stark reality throughout thousands of these small villages. It was their only form of birth control.

Within 50 years of the Roman invasion, infanticide became an everyday event and not only among the impoverished peasants. The more wealthy villa- and land-owners also introduced the practice. The killing of infant boys and girls appears to have been carried out with the full knowledge, permission and understanding of the mothers who accepted that it had become all but impossible to keep, feed, clothe and nurture all their children. In many respects infanticide had become almost a necessity for the extended families came to the conclusion that they were simply unable to care for all their children.

Young women were permitted to keep their first three or four babies and after that their newborn offspring were taken from them. Usually, the newborn babies were sacrificed to one or other of the gods that were worshipped by the village. The sacrifice of babies to the gods was considered an honourable event that brought good fortune to the family and to the village. In other areas, the newborn offspring were taken away and ceremonially drowned in the nearby ponds and streams. It appears that the practice of infanticide came to be accepted in those days of Roman Britain as readily as contraception is accepted in today's society.

The desire by wealthy Britons and landowners to ape their Roman conquerors had a dramatic effect on the import of goods into the country. There was a dramatic upsurge of imported goods as the British aristocracy and aspiring land-owners and traders decided that keeping abreast of the new Roman régime was no longer a luxury but almost a necessity. The importation of luxury articles into Britain by shippers and traders towards the end of the first century was enormous. And this caused a horrendous trade imbalance, the first of many that have continued to the present day.

At that time, Britain produced or possessed very little that could counter-balance the importation of so many luxuries, that included wine and metal work, jewellery and silks. The only trade Britain offered was slaves and some animals, particularly hunting dogs. The metal produced in Britain belonged to the state and did not count as articles of commerce. The peasants' production of wheat, unfettered by the end of tribal warfare, increased but none could be exported because the increase was easily absorbed by the need to supply the Roman Army and officials.

The consequences were a heavy and rapid drainage of money into the pockets of the traders who were mainly foreigners and a heavy burden of debt principally incurred by the highest class of society. Subsequently, they turned to the money-lenders who were mainly foreigners, and incurred more debt. It could not last.

This ruinous state of affairs lasted for some decades as Britain suffered its first serious trade imbalance, accompanied by heavy personal debt. It could not go on. Eventually, the nation's craftsmen and traders came to the rescue. The British craftsmen had over decades built up a good reputation throughout Europe for first-class pottery, woodwork and metalwork. Eventually, these skilled workers began producing the same articles that were being purchased for inflated prices from overseas.

In particular, the British craftsmen began producing

elegant and practical pots and pans for cooking, ironmongery, pottery, as well as highly-prized ornamental objects in bronze and glassware, the glass good enough for window panes. Although the skilled British worker did not replace the foreign traders in respect of the most expensive items, he did, nevertheless, come to produce the great bulk of those objects which were in constant demand.

One of the reasons for the increase in trade across Britain was the Romans' insistence of laying down straight, metalled roads as they had done in France and other conquered territories. The Romans built the roads for speed of movement so that legions could move from one end of a country to the other easily and efficiently. It also speeded the transport of vital goods. Road engineering was carried out by the legions as soon as they had made safe the territory.

One of the principal reasons for the roads lasting for so many centuries were the foundations of layered broken stone and rock. On top of the foundations was laid a layer of fine stone and gravel. Then came the securely laid cobbled stones. Once built, the roads were handed over to local administrators to maintain and this was usually done by prisoners or slaves. In most areas, the gangs were permitted to work freely but in regions of the north, where escape was easy and recapture problematic, the slaves and prisoners were put in chains to prevent their escape.

All the Empire's main roads had post-houses constructed every 15 miles with staging posts and inns every 30 miles. At both the inns and the post-houses the oxen or horses would be fed, watered and quartered, and replaced by another team. It was a most efficient and fast method of transport.

Rome ruled Britain for 400 years through governors who were sent to the islands by the Emperors in Rome. The beginning of the fifth century saw the beginning of the dissolution of the Roman Empire. Rome was opposed by various enemies, the patriotism of Old Rome had faded, her civilisation was decadent, her men effeminate, her intellectuals debased, her statesmen impolitic and her rulers were numerous but divided.

The pressure on Rome's frontiers was ever increasing, and now with enemies on all sides and with civil strife and discord at home, she had relinquished one by one her provinces and slowly surrendered the western parts of her Empire. The legionnaires who had brought peace to Britain for 400 years and defended the island against the plundering vagabonds and invaders were recalled to Rome.

In mainland Europe, the warring barbarian hordes that were swarming over the continent were taking advantage of the withdrawal of the Roman legions. And the Britons who had lived happily and in peace for so long were no longer a nation of fighting men. The men were untrained for combat, the ramparts of stone in the north and the swords of Rome's legionnaires had lulled her into a false sense of security.

Britain had no navy but had relied on Rome's fleet of ships for protection from a constant stream of invaders from the Baltic region. Much of Britain's youth had been slaughtered in their thousands when Roman governors had dispatched untrained young Britons to fight for the Roman

Empire in European wars.

The Celtic Britons offered very little defence against the Teuton invaders — the Saxons, Angles, and Jutes — savage, barbarous men and excellent fighters who worshipped the god of valour.

In desperation, ancient Britons tried to defend their homes, their villages and their handsome towns, but to no avail. Unable to hold back the invaders from Europe, many thousands fled to the hills of Wales and Scotland while others were enslaved to the conquerors. Almost 400 years of Roman culture, which had had such a dramatic effect on the life and habits of the British people, would be virtually destroyed.

BIBLIOGRAPHY

Ancient Authors

Ammianus Marcellinius (cAD330–95), *historia augusta*
Antonine Itinerary (third century)
Appian (cAD90–160)
Augustus, *res gestae* (AD14)
Aurelius Victor (later fourth century), *caesares* or *de caesaribus*
Caesar (100–44BC) *Commentaries on the Gallic War*
'Chronicler of 452' (previously attributed to Prosper Tiro)
Claudian (died c404)
Cassius Dio (later second century to after AD229)
Code of Justinian, *codex justinianus*, issued AD529, revised AD543

Digest of Justinian, (*digesta seu pandectae*, AD533)

Eutropious (mid-fourth century), *brevarium*

Gildas (mid-sixth century), *de excidio et conquestu britanniae*

Herodian (early third century), *Histories*

Justinian (emperor)

notita dignitatum (late fourth/early fifth century)

Orosius (early fifth century), *historiae adversum pagnos*

Panegyrics, *panegyryrici latini veteres, Panegyric of Constantius Caesar* (AD297), *Panegyric of Constantine the Great* (AD297), *Panegyric of Theodosius the Great* (AD389)

Procopius (sixth century), *History of the Wars of Justinian*

Ptolemy (first half of the second century), *Geography*

Ravenna Cosmography (seventh century)

scriptores historiae augustae (late fourth century)

Strabo (mid-first to early second century), *Geography*

Suetonius (later first to early second century), *Lives of the Caesars*

Tacitus (mid-first to early second century), *Tacitus Argicola, Histories, Annals, Theodosian Code* (AD438)

Vegetius (late fourth century)

Verona List (AD312–14)

Zosimus (early sixth century), *Frontier People of Roman Britain*

Modern Authors

Alfoldi A, *Epigraphica* (1940)

Baradez J, *Vue-aerienne de l'organisation romaine dans le sud algerien 'Fossatum Africae'*. Paris (1949)

Barkocsy L, *Beitrage zum Rang der Lagerstadte am Ende des*

II, Anfang des III Jahrhunderts (1953)

Behrens G, *Verschwundene Mainzer Romerbauten* (1954)

Bell H I, *A Latin Registration of Birth* (1937)

Birley E, *An Introduction to the Excavation of Chesterholm-Vindolanda* (1931)

    Excavavations at Chesterholm-Vindolanda (1931)

    A New Inscription from Chesterholm (1934)

    Fourth Report on Excavations at Housesteads (1935)

    Marcus Cocceius Firmus: An Epigraphic Study (1936)

    A Modern Building of Housesteads (1938)

    The Brigantian Problem and the First Roman Contact with Scotland (1950)

    Roman Britain and the Roman Army (1953)

    The Roman Milestone at Middleton in Lonsdale (1954)

    The Hinterland of Hadrian's Wall (1954)

    The Congress of the Roman Frontier Studies (1949)

Bohn O, *Rheinische 'Lagerstadte'* (1926)

Bosanquet R C, *Excavations on the Line of the Roman Wall in Northumberland; the Roman Camp at Housesteads* (1904)

Brogan O, *Trade Between the Roman Empire and the Free Germans* (1936)

Bruce JC, *The Roman Wall* (1867)

Buckland WW, *A Textbook of Roman Law from Augustus to Justinian* (1921 & 1950)

Cheeseman GL, *The Auxilia of the Roman Imperial Army* (1914)

Cichorius C, *Die Reliefs der Traianssaule* (1896–1900)

Clarke J, *Excavations at Milton (Tassieholm) in Season* (1950)

Collingwood RG, *Romano-Celtic Art in Northumbria* (1930),

An Introduction to the Prehistory of Cumberland, Westmoreland and Lancashire North of the Sands (1933)

Collingwood RG, *Prehistoric Settlements near Crosby Ravensworth, The Middleton Milestone*

Collingwood RG and Myres JNL, *Roman Britain and the English Settlements* (1937)

Corder P, *The Reorganization of the Defences of Romano-British Towns in the Fourth Century* (1956)

Corder P and Richmond IA, *Petuaria* (1942)

Curle J, *An Inventory of Objects of Roman and Provincial Roman Origin found on Sites in Scotland and not Definitely Associated with Roman Constructions* (1932)

Domaszewski A Von, *Die Rangordnung des romishcen Heeres* (1908)

Eggar R, *Bemerkungen zum Territorium pannonishcer Festungen* (1952)

Eggars HJ, *Die Romische Import im freien Germanien Hamburg* (1951)

Ellis PB, *The Druids* (1994)

Fair MC, *Roman and Briton. A Theory for Future Establishment of Facts* (1943)

Gillam JP, *Calpurnius Agricola and the Northern Frontier* (1953), *Roman and Native* AD122–197

Haverfield F,   *The Romanization of Roman Britain* (1915)
                 On Julius Verus, A Roman Governor of Britain (1905)

Hawkes CFC, *Britons, Romans and Saxons round Salisbury and in Cranborne Chase* (1948)

Hogg AHA, *The Votadini, in Aspects of Archaeology in Briain and Beyond* (1951)

Holder A, *Alt-Celtischer Sprachschatz, Leipzig* (1896–1907)

Homes TR, *Ancient Britain and the Invasions of Julius Caesar* (1907)

Jacobi L, *Das Romerkastell Saalburg bei Homburg vor der Hohe* (1897)

Jobey G, *Some Rectilinear Settlements of the Roman Period in Northumberland* (1960)

Jolowicz HF, *Historical Introduction to the Study of Roman Law* (1952)

Jorns W, *Die Ausgrabungen am Zugmantel im Herbst* 1953 (1951)

Jorns W and Schleiermacher W, *Das Lagerdorf der Kastells Butzbach*

Kunkel W, *Romisches Privatrecht* (1949)

Laur-Belart R, *Vindonissa, Lager and Vicus* (1953)

Merrix J, *The Buildings of Roman Extramural Settlements and their Occupants*

Millett M, *The Romanisation of Britain (*1990)

Mocsy A, *Das Territorium Legionis und Die Canabe in Pannonien* (1953)

Mommsen T, *Romische Lagerstadte, Gesammelte Schriften* (1910)

Morris J, *The Vallum Again* (1951)

Nash Williams VE, *The Roman Frontier in Wales* (1954)

Nash Williams VE and Nash Williams AH, *Catalogue of the Roman Inscribed and Sculptures Stones found at Caerlon, Monmouthshire* (1935)

Newstead R, *The Roman Station, Prestatyn* (1937)

Petrikovits H Von, *Die Ausgrabungen in der Colonia Traiana bei Zanten* (1952)

> *Ein Ziegelstempel der Cohors II Varcianorum aus Gelduba-Gellep* (1954)
>
> *Vetera, Paulys Realencyclopadie der klassischen Alterumswissenschft* (1958)

Reynolds PJ, *Iron-Age Farm* (1979)

Royal Commission on Ancient Monuments (Scotland) (1956)

Richmond IA, *Excavations on Hadrian's Wall in the Birdoswald-Pike Hill Sector* (1929)

> *The Roman Fort at South Shields* (1934)
>
> *The Sarmatae* (1945)
>
> *Roman Settlement* (1949)
>
> *The Roman Fort at South Shields* (1953)
>
> *Queen Cartimandua* (1954)
>
> *Roman Britain* (1955)

Richmond IA, *Roman and Native in North Britain* (1958)

Richmond IA and Crawford OGS, *The British Section of the Ravenna Cosmography* (1949)

Robertson AS, *An Antonine Fort: Golden Hill, Duntocher* (1957)

St Joseph JK, *Air Reconnaissance of North Britain* (1951)

Salway P, *Roman Britain* (1981), *The Frontier People of Roman Britain* (1965)

Schauer W, *Doctoral dissertation*

Schonberger H, *Plan zu Ausgrabungen am Kastell Zugmantel bis zum Jahre 1950* (1952)

Schulten A, *Das Territorium Legionis Hermes* (1894)

Schulz F, *Roman Registers of Births and Death Certificates* (1942–43)

Seeck O, *Notitia Dignitataum, Berlin* (1876)

Sherwin-White AN, *The Roman Citizenship* (1939)

Steer KA, *Roman and Native in North Britain: The Severan Reorganisation in Roman and Native in North Britain The Antonine Wall 1934–59*

Stevenson GH, *Roman Provincial Administration till the Age of the Antonines* (1939)

Stone G, *England — From the Earliest Times to the Great Charter* (1916)

Straub A, *Les Canabenses et l'Origine de Strasbourg* (1886)

Swinbank B, *The Vallum Reconsidered* (1954)

Swoboda E, *Carnuntum, seine Geschichte und seine Denkmaler* (1953)

Szilagyi J, *Aquincum* (1956)

Van Griffen AE, *Drie Romeinse Terpen, Jaaverslag van de Vereinigung vooe Terpenonderzoek* (1948)

Vorbeck E, *Militarinscriften aus Carnuntum* (1954)

Wheeler REM (Sir Mortimer), *The Roman Fort near Brecon* (1926)

Wilmanns G, *Die Romische Lagerstadt Afrikas in Commentationes philologae in honorem Theodori Mommseni* (1877)

Wlassak M, *Zum Romischen Provinzialprozess* (1919)

Woelcke K, *Die Neue Stadtplan von Nida-Heddernheim* (1938)

Wright RP, *The Establishment of the Fort at Chester-le-Street in AD216* (1944)